Acclaim for Deborah Digges's

The Stard...

"*The Stardust Lounge* is s̲...   ...utifully
written. For anyone concer...   ...ne who
plans a family, anyone who ...   ...animals—this book
is a must. I was caught up in the drama; I could not put it down."
                                              —Jane Goodall

"Well crafted, quite stunning at times. . . . So idiosyncratic and
strangely moving that if it were fiction it would seem contrived beyond critical description."   —*The Washington Post*

"[One] of the best confessional memoirs this year."
                                    —*St. Louis Post-Dispatch*

"A wrenching memoir about the things that mothers and children
will do to, and for, one another, written with a poet's eye for resonant images."   —*Booklist*

"Deborah Digges has written a memoir so powerfully charged and
exquisitely textured that I found it transcended its medium and
drew me unequivocally into its world, as only the best books do."
                                        —Nicholas Christopher

"The rest of the world may suffer from blindness and prejudice toward the most interesting children and animals but Digges sees
them clearly, likes them for what they are and refuses to abandon
them to a hostile world. If everyone could be the kind of parent
that she is the world would be a far better place."
                                    —Elizabeth Marshall Thomas

Deborah Digges

The Stardust Lounge

Deborah Digges is the author of the memoir *Fugitive Spring* and three award-winning volumes of poetry. Her poetry appears regularly in *The New Yorker* and other publications. She lives in Massachusetts with her husband, Frank.

The

Stardust

Lounge

ANCHOR BOOKS
A Division of Random House, Inc.
New York

The
Stardust
Lounge

**STORIES FROM A
BOY'S ADOLESCENCE**

Deborah Digges

**WITH PHOTOGRAPHS
BY STEPHEN DIGGES**

FOR FRANK

and in memory of my father

FIRST ANCHOR BOOKS EDITION, MAY 2002

Copyright © 2001 by Deborah Digges

The Library of Congress has cataloged the Nan A. Talese/Doubleday edition as follows:
Digges, Deborah.
The Stardust Lounge : stories from a boy's adolescence / Deborah Digges; with photographs by Stephen Digges.
p. cm.
ISBN 0-385-50158-7
1. Digges, Stephen—Childhood and youth. I. Title.
CT275.D464 A3 2001
973.9'092—dc21
[B]
2001017181

Anchor ISBN: 0-385-72093-9

Author photograph © Stephen Digges
Book design by Pei Loi Koay

www.anchorbooks.com

Printed in the United States of America
10 9 8 7 6 5 4 3 2

There are no laws in the air.

The

Stardust

Lounge

Stephen on the stoop, 1991

Midday, midsummer. Iowa City. Stephen and I are waiting for our clothes to dry at the Bloomington Street Laundromat. Charles is away at summer camp.

When we arrived at the laundry, unloaded our baskets, and hauled them inside we heard something familiar, the clear, resonant sound of a cello, a young man practicing while his clothes go through the washer and dryer.

The first time we discovered the cellist at the Laundromat this past fall, twelve-year-old Charles had been undone with excitement. "Mom," he'd whispered to me, "this is a painting! I've got to do some sketches!"

As the cellist plays, the few of us here are listening—the attendant, an older couple passing through. In the parking lot their Airstream trailer glints in the sun. Its license plates read Idaho.

Just outside the entrance five-year-old Stephen enacts a game in which, from time to time, he whirls and crouches,

*brandishing his favorite blanket at an imaginary foe. A
flock of sparrows anting in the dust nearby rises and circles
and resettles each time he sweeps close to them.*

*I fold the boys' bright shirts and shorts, our old, comfort-
able towels, mismatched socks, an ordinary activity made
sacred in light of the music. The cellist plays through to
the end of a piece. Then he sets his instrument aside and
unloads his clothes from the dryer.*

*As I ready to carry our baskets to the car, the woman of
the Airstream trailer comes over to me and touches my arm.*

*"Is that your little boy?" she asks, nodding toward Ste-
phen, who kneels now, quiet in the strangeness of the silence
the music created. He stares toward the sparrows taking
wings full of dust into their feathers.*

"Yes," I answer. "His name is Stephen."

*"He's—" She stops. "There is something special about
him, isn't there? I've been watching him. May I lay my
hand on his head?"*

*I must look confused, because the woman offers quickly,
"My husband and I are both professors of parapsychol-
ogy. We study psychic phenomena. We've been traveling
across country on a lecture tour. Now we're on our way
home..."*

"I see," I offer, trying to hide my skepticism.

"My name is Beth. What's yours?"

"Deborah."

"Is it all right if I touch him?"

"If Stephen doesn't mind."

*"Stephen?" the woman says softly as she moves toward
him and kneels. "Stephen, my name is Beth." She places her
hand on his head.*

"Hi, Beth," Stephen says easily. "I'm Thteve." He smiles, revealing his missing teeth as he looks into her face.

As I see it, the stars were once nameless, and the days and the months of the year. Then they had many names, the names we gave them and forgot and misremembered. They fell in and out of their own timing, the seasons particular to the angle of the light, the pitch of the planet—by the laws of gravity earth's one moon decided the tides.

Maybe with people it is different. Certain people emanate something other, some newness, time or timelessness. They enlighten or shadow others. It is in them and little gets in its way.

So it is with a woman named Beth and a child with a lisp who calls himself Thteve at the threshold of the Laundromat one summer day in Iowa, a moment I'll remember, a moment so many others will fall into to lose themselves or find direction.

Beth is kneeling. She is laying her hand on my son's blond head and nodding. "Oh, yes," she says as she smooths his hair and stands. She touches my arm. "Deborah—your Stephen? He'll know a higher turn in the spiral."

Stephen in Iowa, 1983

Thirteen-year-old Stephen has run away again. He's out there somewhere with his gang, all of them dressed for the dark in black-hooded sweatshirts, oversized team jackets, ball caps, baggy pants that ride low on their hips. Inside their pockets they hold on to guns, switchblades. Recently Stephen has shaved part of his right eyebrow.

It's about 4:00 A.M., late September. I'm in my study on the east side of our brownstone apartment house in Brookline, Massachusetts, three stories above the street.

Maybe Stephen can see that my study light is on. I imagine him looking up from one of the condemned train cars' shot-out windows in the rubble field not far from us, looking up to this coin of light like a lighthouse beacon in one of my mother's favorite hymns.

But Stephen would protest he is no flailing ship. He is Henry Martin, the youngest of three brothers in the Scottish ballad I used to read to him, Henry Martin, who became the robber of the three, having drawn the losing lot.

But as fate would have it, Martin was good at pirating—brutal, unequivocal, the beloved captain of a ship that cruised the shoals off Britain, pillaging shipwrecks and intercepting inbound merchant vessels.

All night in Boston sirens close in, scale back. We are as far north as we have ever been, the light here opening on a series of stingy, frigid days, shutting down suddenly.

Maybe the cops have picked Stephen up, in which case I will hear something soon. More likely he has fallen asleep on the floor of someone's room. It might be hours before I hear from him. He has run enough times that I know he will call. He hates himself for having to, but he can't help it. When he hears my voice he will be profane.

It's cold in my study, cold throughout our rooms. Stunningly beautiful is our apartment, but cold, often barely fifty-five degrees. But cold as it is, the oil bills are enormous, midwinter, half my salary.

I'd build a fire but this would mean my taking the back stairs to the yard, opening a common door. We are in enough trouble. Our landlords, who live below us, call often these days to tell Stephen to turn down the rap music. And sometimes he brings his gang home, ten or more boys stomping up the front flight of stairs.

Then there are the shouting matches between Stephen and his older brother, between Stephen and his stepfather, Stan, who visits when he can, these days about every third weekend.

And there are the shouting matches between Stephen and me. They get us nowhere despite my wailing, begging, and then my sudden turns from despair to fury that find me chasing after him down the stairs, out the double doors and over the back wall, up the eighty or so steps to the car.

At forty I am amazed at my speed, my skill. But Stephen is faster. Just recently he has outgrown me by a few inches. By the time I reach the landing lot, he and my car are gone.

In my study near dawn I turn back to a grant proposal I've been working on while I wait for word from the cops or from my son. If I could get a semester off from teaching, I'd have the time and concentration to move us out of here, find a place outside the city far enough that Stephen couldn't get in, close enough that I could commute to the university.

I refuse to entertain the impossible logistics, all the binding clauses, and how broke I am. I owe the landlords for oil, and the electric and phone companies, owe Stephen's therapist, and a lousy therapist at that. Or maybe it is that no one can help us just now.

I'm also looking at a huge tuition bill for spring term at the private school we placed Stephen in a year ago. We hoped a change would help, the smaller classes, and the "positive peer group," the "family atmosphere" the school promised.

But the new school has made things worse. Stephen's circle of friends has widened. They live all over greater Boston, from Wellesley to Mattapan to Beacon Hill, and as usual, Stephen has attracted the most spirited and rebellious.

Weekends they rove the city on public transportation or

in taxis, buy expensive clothes for each other on Newbury Street, score dope in Harvard Square, then hole up in someone's absent parents' Beacon Hill apartment where they smoke, make phone calls, and experiment with their bodies while they watch the parents' stash of X-rated videos.

Perhaps such unsupervised activity has gone on for a long time, before Stephen entered the school, and nothing more than the fact of decadent boredom has come of it. The kids get high, order carryout, mess around, come down.

Then it's getting late. They hop in taxis again and go home, eat with the family, do their homework, go to bed. No one asks where they've been or what they did today. Or if asked, the kids lie. No one misses the money they spent, or cares that they spent it.

That Stephen has become part of the group is to them neither here nor there, except that as he participates he hates it, not because it's wrong or dangerous, but because he can't recover from it.

It is not in his nature to be noncommittal, to dip, unaffected, in and out of worlds. He can't play the game and then go home as if nothing had happened. If he spends his allowance money he has none. If he gets high he gets depressed and sick. And when asked what he did all day, his difficulty with lying makes him hostile, silent.

He hates himself for his vulnerabilities, for his lack of impulse control, for how sick he feels after the dope, and for the fact that he can't keep up, like the others, with his academic work.

But to quit would mean losing his peers. What would he do without them? How would he function without his friends? Because he is doing poorly in his classes and refuses to play team sports of any kind, he believes he has nothing else but this circle of friends he judges and resents.

As for his mother, she's in his face all the time. She tries to get him to "talk about things," sends him to a therapist—another secret he's got to try to keep from his friends. It's her fault he's in this situation. Isn't she the one who insisted he enroll in the Park School where his failures have now so drastically come to light? She deserves to be lied to, lied to, shut out, punished.

Stephen will not quit his friends, though as far as he can tell, they don't have his dilemmas. Were he to confide in them, they'd surely laugh.

Stephen begins to befriend and be befriended by the kids who deal the drugs, the ones who sneer at this entourage of adolescent rich, kids willing to use them for their money and their naïveté. And after a while Stephen finds that he has the power to play one group against the other. When the dealers and their gangs begin to coerce the entourage for expensive gifts, steal from them, bully them, Stephen acts as mediator, savior. He is playing with fire, but the risk is exhilarating.

So much so that at the end of the day, as Stephen's classmates head home, he stays on the streets with his new companions, as angry and confused and as full of self-loathing as ever, but now somehow more in control.

I'm keeping my own secrets regarding a sense of fear and failure. I, too, am torn between identities. I have been a snob, a bohemian snob who believed that the arts, music, poetry were religion enough by which to raise my sons and that somehow, above all the groups in culture—rich and poor alike—we were superior in our passionate pursuits.

I have judged Stephen's new friends; moreover, their parents in their business suits and furs, who speak to me coolly, if at all, on the occasions when I have visited the school on Parents' Night, or to watch Stephen perform his censored raps in the talent show. Their children play flat, dispassionate Bach on the violin. One girl, dressed as a pauper, sings badly, "Wouldn't It Be Loverly?"

At the same time, I have tried to mold Stephen to "fit in" here. Night after night I have done Stephen's home-work, listed the phylum, class, order, genus, species. Mimicking the hand of my thirteen-year-old, I've written notes on his history text, mapped the Nile, made up a rap for him of the capitals, while Stephen, having disappeared up those steps again, spray-paints his tag on another mailbox, climbs a fire escape to put up a piece, a wall of graffiti that will chide greater Boston on its way to work.

And while I have always been an advocate of the underprivileged, the ones in culture most in need, I have to admit to myself now that, well, I guess I didn't mean it *this* way. I didn't mean, for instance, that Stephen should befriend street kids, bring them up into our apartment and feed them and give them his clothes, his watch, his bed. That's not what I meant. But what *did* I mean?

Other self-condemning words go round, culture's words for Stephen and me, words I read on the faces of the Park School parents and their children, *dysfunctional, enabling*, words I've heard Stan say over the telephone. Frustrated, he tells me that I've never been strict enough with my sons and that now I am paying the price.

And I hear the same frustration from my family as they bemoan the fact that I've brought up my sons without organized religion. They offer that perhaps we've moved around the country too much and that this has bred an unhealthy alliance—perhaps I am too much a friend to my boys, not enough *mother*. Implicit in their words is the slap of the fact of my divorce from my sons' father, my marriage to Stan, our commuting relationship.

And because they love Stephen and me they offer advice. One of my sisters suggests a school she has looked into where troubled children like Stephen are dealt with through highly structured days, lots of sports, severe consequences for their actions. "Hip restriction," she explains. "It means kids have with them at all times one of the school staff, wherever they go."

I've looked into such a school located in western Massachusetts. But such schools cost twenty-five to thirty thousand a year, almost a year's salary for me. And when I try to imagine Stephen under those circumstances, I see him in his infancy, a baby so violently undone if I left him that I gave up my teaching assistantship in California to stay home with him.

Then there is the "Tough Love" approach, which Stan offers as a solution. This idea costs nothing. According to its policies one simply locks one's child out, calls the police if there is a disturbance, and hopes the world beats the kid up enough that he begs to come home on any terms.

But this approach to our problems is absurd. It is too dangerous to do such a thing to a thirteen-year-old. Better than anyone, I know Stephen, know that he *would* get lost, would in his anger and despair take some risk that would very likely kill him. I'm not willing to take such a chance with my son.

"You just won't give him up," Stan offers.

"This isn't about you," others suggest.

In the end, I agree with both assessments. I won't give him up and it isn't about me. Sometimes there is no language for what a mother knows about her child. Because there are no words, no argument, it is as if the matter should be taken away from her.

Stephen's therapist doesn't seem to have any particular solution in mind, and though I don't feel he is doing Stephen any good, his approach to our dilemma seems the most appropriate.

"He's angry." Mike states the obvious after each session. "Do your best to keep him out of jail."

Outside, the streetlights and the dim Boston sunrise are almost equal to each other. Light swallows light. Stephen's name means *crowned*.

I see him clearly just now in memory, a boy of about six, scrambling up rocks to a high plateau. The winds off the Atlantic are fierce. We have come to Tintagel to show him King Arthur's castle, a magnificent ruin off the Cornwall coast. He has run, as always, out ahead of me.

The wind carries off my voice as I call to him to wait. But he has disappeared up the rocks and over the rise. Panicked, I clamor after him, lose my footing, recover. The winds shoulder me against the rock face. Where is Stephen? What if he is blown off into the sea?

I heave myself up to the table of green meadow. Out of breath, half-blinded by sea spray, I glimpse the boy running wide circles around the ruins, his arms open, his face lifted to the elements. He is shouting, running, lost to something, in thrall to its dangerous joy.

What if Stephen *is* a Henry Martin, in the end an outlaw? If he is, do I stop loving him? And how do I go about withdrawing my love? It appears that is what humans do in crisis. We pull away. Stan and I have done it. We are doing it now. We don't touch, make love, laugh.

I contend it must be different with a child.

Maybe Stephen believes he is Henry Martin, or he is Odysseus duping the Cyclops, sneaking out of the cave wearing animal skins, crouching among the sheep herds as he leads his crew toward the ship; Stephen, my Ishmael, wild, street-smart, strident, swaggering, who has learned to use his anger and his terror like a weapon and won excellence in the bow shot.

Now the phone rings. "Fuck you," he greets me. Sirens close in again, recede.

"Will you be home soon?"

"Maybe, maybe not," he spits, but the fight has gone out of him. He sounds so very tired.

"Okay. Come on. Watch your back. I'll put on some coffee."

We like to drive around. At the hour when fathers and mothers arrive home from work, at the hour when my own father used to pull into our driveway, the boys and I get in our car and set out on an adventure. We drive happily against traffic, the outbound lanes open to us.

In Missouri and Iowa we drive into the country. The fields, spring through autumn, spin columns of dust in the wake of tractors. In winter, barn doors are shut against the cold. We imagine the animals feeding now. In their hair, coats, caretakers carry with them animal smells through screen doors and into kitchens.

By November the fields are frozen, by January snow-covered, at this hour the furrows holding on to grates of light. The ponds are near circles of sky-colored light like windows shining out of the earth.

Silos are lighthouses over still seas, the pig sheds scattered down the hillsides, houses washed out to sea.

There are certain abandoned farms we find. Sometimes we stop and walk the grounds looking for horseshoes, bottles, sheep's wool to take home with us. If the places are deserted, we let ourselves in the house and walk around trying to pick up some sense of the ghosts whose shoes scored this green linoleum. Who once dragged a soiled hand along rose wallpaper all the way up the stairs? Whose rooms looked out on the road, and did they dream of traveling?

As if the house were ours, we choose bedrooms, invent a life, invent our days. At upstairs windows we look out over miles of meadow and speculate on the hours of work required to keep up so many acres.

Stephen loves the barns and wants to know what animals lived here. He gets down and smells the ground. "Horses" he says, "and lots of dogs."

In one house we find a growing chart for three children, their sizes penciled up along the threshold between the kitchen and what must have been a dining room.

We lived in California long enough to chart eight years of Charles's height, the kitchen door frames in the years prior—Missouri, his birthplace, and then Texas—showing three and one respectively.

Stephen's first height was recorded late—at the age of three—on the kitchen door frame of what is now his father's house.

In the years 1982 to 1985 we live in Iowa. Many family farms have gone under, foreclosure signs leaning against stop signs along the highways.

One farmhouse in particular we love to visit because on

approach you can see through east front window to back west window to sky. When we approach the house at evening—huge, empty—the sun, framed and focused, flares like a furnace fed on stars.

We can't say exactly what engages us. We describe it each time by simile. Stephen says it looks like going to heaven. Charles says that to live there must be like living on a train—Charles, who prefers to sleep on the living room couch with his shoes on.

I've tried to be strict with him about this. "You're thirteen. It's not like you work the night shift. You need to sleep in a bed. In pajamas. Why don't you sleep in your bed?"

"I need to be ready if anything happens," he answers.

"What could happen? Honey, you're safe here."

"I know I'm safe. It's you and Steve I'm talking about."

"We're safe too . . ."

Charles looks at the floor.

"Well, at least take off your shoes? It worries me."

"Can't do it, Mom," he finishes with such authority that I let it go.

But I move Steve's bed into the living room and each night, take to reading to him there. Charles pretends to study, but I can tell he enjoys the stories.

Or he paints, having set up his easel by the west window, paints oil after oil of empty rooms, closed barbershops, gas stations, bus terminals, farmhouses whose windows you can see through to sky.

After some months, he begins to take off his shoes to sleep, though he sleeps fully clothed on the couch in Iowa, later England, and then Maryland. Finally in Boston he seems to make peace with a bed, probably because he chose a couch-bed for his room.

His first autumn in Iowa Charles finishes about thirty paintings. We stretch the canvases ourselves, or when we can't afford canvas Charles gessoes over his earliest efforts, or over a fine piece of wood we've found on our adventures.

The year before, Stephen and I moved from Columbia, Missouri, to the house on Market Street where I attend the Writers Workshop. Then Charles was hesitant to come with us. He chose to stay with his father and his father's new wife in the house we had moved to from California after eight years in the air force.

It has taken coercing to get Charles to join us in Iowa City, coercing I feel guilt about. But I believe my boys should be with me. I believe that they should be together, and that they should be with me.

Never mind that I have only a seven-hundred-and-forty-dollar-a-month teaching assistantship stipend for us to live on, a rented roof to put over our heads. The good news—no taxes will be taken out of my salary because even a year's earning keeps us below the poverty line.

To get us started, pay for an apartment, and enroll Stephen in the Iowa City Montessori school, I receive some equity out of the Columbia house and I sell our micro bus for forty-five hundred dollars, the dealership throwing in a black 1970 Volkswagen Beetle. Charles calls it the getaway car.

At the time of the move from Missouri to Iowa Charles is twelve. In the previous two years he has made the difficult transition from Southern California, where he's spent most of his childhood, to the middle of Missouri.

Now I'm asking him to move again, this time without his father for whom he is named, and for whom he pined all the years of his father's flying out over the Pacific on months-long sorties in the air force.

Charles is being asked to move away again in a tiny old car to which is attached a U-Haul trailer that slows our speed, even on the interstate, to twenty-five miles an hour.

I have a poor memory for the year that Charles isn't with Stephen and me. I'm ashamed at our circumstances, at the wrecked marriage. When people ask if Stephen is my only son I say yes, dreading a muddled explanation as to why Charles doesn't live with us.

Stephen misses his father and brother, too. So we begin weekend drives to meet halfway, Charles and his father coming as far as Bloomfield, Iowa, Stephen and I meeting them there on Friday evenings under the bank light on Bloomfield's small town square. We try to time those drives so that no one waits long, Stephen and I traveling south on two-lane back roads through Iowa farmland.

In the warm weather we keep all the windows down, smell the livestock, the black earth, watch as great flocks of starlings, grackles, crows explode before us.

In the tiny town of St. Francisville we pay a nickel to cross the bridge.

If we arrive early, Stephen plays with his matchbox cars on the town green. In cold weather we stay in the car, the engine idling to keep the heat coming. When Charles and his father arrive, the four of us walk over to a café.

The initial meetings are difficult. But they get easier.

In spite of the problems that led us to divorce, Charles Senior and I have always liked each other. I'm glad to see him.

We shake hands and take the son in our arms who lives with the other. Into our futures as the parents of our sons—the only children either of us will ever have—we seem to agree in silence that dignity and kindness, however strained, is the best course of action. There will be graduations, accidents, prizes, weddings, and funerals we are bound to attend in the other's presence because of our boys.

The trauma of the divorce is behind us, not without leaving scars. But we figure, without saying so, that neither of us can extract the last thirteen years of our lives.

We're part of each other, part of the other's youth. And the boys will grow into traits and habits resembling each of us—Charles will inherit my love of books and my bent toward brooding, his father's good nature and the Digges ego, Stephen my spontaneity, which can turn quickly to impulsiveness, his father's fair beauty and single-mindedness.

During those first weeks and months in which we meet in Bloomfield, I suspect we find a way to continue to love the other in our children.

Then under the bank light's dropping temperature we say good-bye, set out again in different directions. Sometimes Stephen and I take his brother with us back to Iowa City for the weekend. Sometimes Stephen goes with his dad, Charles with me, and still other times, Stephen goes back for the weekend with his father and brother.

Such an arrangement is in place one autumn evening as Stephen and I drive south again to meet Charles and his father. We've set out later than usual. We're in a hurry. During the hilly climb out of Iowa City the car groans and backfires.

Once we're on level ground it seems better, but at the main intersection in Ottumwa, about thirty miles from Bloomfield, the Volkswagen throws a rod and dies at the stoplight.

In 1983 few people I know own telephone answering machines, and if they do, those early machines haven't the feature that make calling in to pick up messages possible. In the middle of traffic I put on the flashers and Stephen and I set off down the road.

In a phone booth I find the number of a local garage, and once I know they're on their way to the car, dial Charles's number in Columbia. How I'm to pay for the tow and the repairs I haven't figured yet.

I have to call, collect, Charles' new wife, Terri, and I'm grateful to hear her voice as she accepts the charges.

"Why don't you just rent a car?" Terri suggests when I tell her our circumstances.

"I don't have a credit card," I answer.

"No credit card?"

"No. Listen. Surely Charles will call when we don't arrive. Could I ask you to tell him where we are?"

"Where are you?"

I'm looking down the street. Everything is shut up, closed for the night. But about a mile down the road, back toward Iowa City, we'd passed a motel, its restaurant as I remember called the Stardust Lounge.

"We'll be waiting at the Stardust Lounge."

"You're kidding." Terri laughs.

"Tell Charles it's right on the interstate beyond Ottumwa. Tell him to look for a pink neon sign with yellow stars . . ."

The first night I shadow Stephen, I watch his direction from our balcony, then tiptoe down the stoop into the brisk early December air. I keep the hood of his sweatshirt tied tightly, my hair tucked in a stocking cap underneath.

At about a block's distance, hugging the stone wall down Winthrop Road, he heads toward the T-stop. I feel giddy and must suppress a nearly overwhelming urge to call out to Stephen, as if, outside the arena of our discord, we could meet and embrace, set out together in compatible alignment.

As he boards a southbound train, I look at my watch: 12:45. I've planned badly. I have no money, no contingency plan for a taxi after the trains have stopped for the night, no way of knowing where he'll get off—though I suspect Hyde Park or Mattapan—and no idea of how I might change trains, board or exit without being discovered.

Against my will something like admiration steals over me. How well Stephen has learned to navigate the night. He'd boarded that train with presence approaching dignity, offered his token to the conductor, and taken his seat like a veteran. Walking back up the hill I wonder at the chasm that has opened between us. How have we assigned each other so distinctly to different worlds? And is it, to Stephen, even personal? Or does it only become personal—and volatile—when I, assigned to represent the tedium of the day life, try to coax him back. It's *fun* out here in the dark, I agree. It's strange and awakening now to find my way through the cold past tomorrow's garbage pickup, past the almost salvageable chairs, an entire set of windows, an old doll house I am tempted to retrieve and take home.

Fighting a temptation toward anger at Stephen's refusal to apply his mastery to anything but deviant activities, I remind myself to just observe for now. Observe and learn. I remember a passage from Jane Goodall's *In the Shadow of Man*, a passage I've written down in my journal: *When the frustrations of being with individuals so dominant... become too great, the adolescent male [chimp] travels...frequently by himself.... This aloneness is quite deliberate....*

I've turned to many texts to try to learn how best to understand Stephen. Most if not all the psychology books are either briefly vague on adolescence, or they discuss the problem theoretically or in regard to two-parent families. There is a good deal of information on behavior modification, but none of the texts explain what it feels like to be an adolescent boy.

I first read Goodall's accounts of her studies of chimpanzees years ago, sitting in the bleachers, watching
Stephen's soccer practices. I'd written his name, Charles,
and mine in the margins of the text as I'd read about the
various behaviors of young chimps in relationship to their
mothers, siblings, and the community at large.

Among other similarities, the strong, solitary bond between a mother chimp and her offspring—independent
of the adult males in the community—seemed pertinent
to us. Just as the adult males live in wide orbit around
female chimps and their young, so the boys' father and
stepfather have always lived on the far edges of our
lives.

My boys' father flew planes in the air force. We lived
parallel to the base's east-west runway, the huge C-141's
taking off and landing morning, noon, and night. Stephen was born into a family in which, from the day he
entered the world, he watched his father come and go.

My marriage to Stan is in many ways no different.
For five of our six years together, we've maintained two
residences, he living and working in Maryland and I
in Boston.

Sitting high in the bleachers over Brookline's playing
fields, watching my small son run with his teammates,
knowing my older boy painted or read at home, I had
starred a passage: *The behavior of some human males is
not so different from chimpanzee males as might be expected. In the Western world, at any rate, many fathers,
even though they may be materially responsible for their
families' welfare, spend much time away from their wives
and children—often in the company of other men....*

Goodall's writings about the chimps at Gombe helped me come to terms with and value my singleness. Invested with a more anthropological and philosophical view of our one-parent household, I attempted to peel away the many-layered fiction of American family life and the eighties consensus view that single mothering was somehow a new and aberrant condition.

When did men not go to sea, to war, set out on seasonal hunts, get lost, die of smallpox, malaria, die in the woods with handwritten wills frozen to their chests? When did they not board ships for a new world, secure a place on a wagon train going west? Were the months-, often years-long absences irrelevant to their children's lives? Sanctioned or not by traditional values, isn't absence still absence? And through those absences, who fed the children, sang to them? Under whose single care might we document that we grew?

As Stephen enters such a troubled adolescence, I've found myself poring over Goodall's book once more in regard to the behavior of adolescent chimps: *Adolescence is a difficult and frustrating time for some chimpanzees just as it is for some humans. Possibly it is worse for males in both species.... One of the most stabilizing factors for the adolescent male may well be his relationship to his mother....*

A few nights later, the door softly closes and I pull on again the black sweatshirt and pants from Stephen's drawer. Just now he and I are almost the same height and weight. I've tucked some money in my sock, but tonight Stephen cuts down the terraced steps toward Washington Street and past the T-stop. He wears his backpack and I can hear the ball bearings rattling in the paint cans as he bounces down the long flight of stairs.

I follow him at a distance along Beacon, he on one side of the street, I on the other. I keep to the shadows of the awninged storefronts. To my relief Stephen is listening to his Walkman, which gives me greater ease in my movements. I can follow a bit closer without worrying that he'll hear me.

At the same time the fact of his rather distractedly bouncing down the street makes me evermore protective. Someone could jump him and he'd never know what hit him. I scan the streets, the openings to the many alleys. Stephen leads toward Boston. As I dart and stroll, hesitate when he is too clearly in view, I feel a strong pull toward home. Does Stephen feel anything like it? He certainly doesn't appear to.

We are almost to Fenway when he cuts left onto St. Mary's Street. At the corner two kids about his age step out of the convenience store. Stephen stops and removes his headphones. There's an exchange. On the spot I decide that if violence erupts, I'll blow my cover, step in.

Though I know I can't stop a fight all by myself, I'm banking on the surprise factor, pulling off my hood and cap, shaking out my hair to reveal myself as *mother on the scene.... When he is attacked ... there is little a mother can do, but she usually hurries to see what is going on, and may utter* waa *barks in the background....*

But the boys join Stephen as they make their way behind the apartments, stopping at a fence to toss part of a Slim Jim to a dog. Maybe the boys feed the dog to keep him from barking. Stephen kneels a moment. He reaches

his fingers through the wire mesh fence and scratches
the animal on his head. Then the boys head off again toward Commonwealth, cross the viaduct, and disappear.
Crouching along the rail, a few cars whizzing by beneath,
I follow.

When I reach the other side, I peer down the path
between high dead weeds to an old trestle. Even from a
distance, in the midst of the rubble grown up around it,
the trestle retains something of the baroque vision of its
builders, elaborate scrolls and buttresses written into the
behemoth stone and concrete structure.

Here and there off the path, the homeless have erected
low, tarp-covered houses. Just now no one stirs. They're either asleep or roaming. I can feel my pulse in my tem-
ples—*I set off one morning for the mountain . . .*—and
squat to catch my breath as I behold the enormous ruin.

Something like gunshots followed by laughter brings
me to my feet as I sprint down the path and flatten myself against the outside wall. It is like looking into an
enormous tortoise shell, or a cave whose entrance your
head barely clears, then opens before you like a cathe-
dral.

I can see that the explosions are the result of ignited
spray cans flaring to small fires along tracks that run the
length of the enclosure. The litter of fires from one end
of the trestle to the other creates enough light that the
ten or eleven boys there, including Stephen, take to
clowning in front of them, casting huge shadows on the
opposite walls like the shadows of the carriers behind the
screen in Plato's Allegory of the Cave.

And I can't help thinking of the caves of Lascaux as I

take in the huge, colorful paintings, many of them elegies as I observe, elegies for friends who have been shot, or died of overdoses, or who, as the captions read, were *sent up da riva to juvie.*

Obscenities, rap lyrics—*fuck da police, bum rush the show*, and *a little somtin fo da younstas*—are brandished in black under the faces of the dead. Valiant swan songs, ballooned speech announces *see ya lata* and *live and let live2X.*

The walls are a swarm of tags overlaid, painted out, rewritten, and resurfacing, secret names the boys have given themselves or their gangs. Tags ladder the walls like a catalogue of ships, or a roll call to something—to arms, to the New Jerusalem—the effect of their numbers glorious, disturbing.

The boys choose names of one or two syllables, perhaps because they are easier to remember, or because of the hammer-blow of the sound. They spell their tags phonetically, as if to translate as far away from culture as possible without losing meaning, tags like *abuz, sez, chek, beepr, alirt, myo, hed*, and many, many others scrawled elaborately across the walls and up to the dank, green-to-black mildewed ceiling arcing at thirty or forty feet.

I slide a bit on the steep embankment, find my footing. But I'm undetected in the shadows outside the abutments, the traffic sounds, amplified inside the tunnel, covering the noise of my bumbling in the weeds as every now and then I glance behind me to the cardboard houses, then peer around the wall to watch Stephen, at the far end of the trestle, unload his backpack of paint cans.

He lights a few empties to the delight of his comrades.

His laughter, so childlike, so catching, sounds both liber-
ating and exclusive, as if I'd stumbled into the wrong
dream. The cans hiss, spray fire like heavy rain that
weirdly illuminates the floors littered with freebase
lids, broken syringes, homemade bongs, rolling papers.

Stephen begins squaring off a section of wall with
white paint and fills it in, creating for himself a field.
Then he backs away to let it dry. The exhilaration of the
night's discoveries begins to dissipate in waves of dizzy
fatigue as I survey the scene. Paint fumes hit my nostrils and I step back in the dark.

Drawing of guns by Stephen Digges, age 5

Christmas Eve, 1991. We are passionately pretending at
normal. Charles is home from college, in his room wrapping presents, listening to Mozart. Stephen is "at a
friend's" until seven, when we intend to have our holiday
dinner. Stan is here, in the bedroom reading. Against his
wishes I've asked a few of Stephen's friends, albeit possible gang members, and their mothers to stop by before
dinner for holiday drinks and treats.

The turkey's in the oven. Things smell good. I have
just finished wrapping gifts and set them under our enormous tree—as if the size of a tree could make up for the
emptiness we feel—and I am setting a fine table. Against
the Mozart there are carols on the radio. The collision is
lovely; between the iambic of the carols runs Mozart,
bodiless, into the high octaves.

A week ago tonight Stephen was booted unequivocally
from his private school. He had brought a gun with him

one morning with the purpose of scaring, he said, a girl. He alleged that the girl had threatened to turn him in to a rival gang.

She was angry with Stephen because he'd slept through one of her 3:00 A.M. taxi rides in from Newton to our apartment. Apparently she'd even thrown rocks at his bedroom window. So, he hadn't shown up for what must have been some sort of tryst, or drug deal.

I'm acquainted with the girl because one night this past October she ran away, in a taxi, to our house. Disheveled, she wept that her father had beaten her. I'd called the police, then the girl's parents. The father and the police met in our apartment. After much conversing—in my bedroom with the door closed—the police sent the girl and her father home.

But she'd called again moments later, this time from her father's car phone. She cried for help. I was suspicious. Was she, in fact, being beaten? I could hear her father's voice pleading, practical.

The thought police would surely have me on this one: A child claims she is being abused, and I suspect she is lying? At the same time I doubted that the cops, in a ten-minute chat in my bedroom, had got at the truth.

Once more I called the police, who tracked down the girl and her father, pulled them over. Once again the police released them.

As it turned out, the gun Stephen had packed to school was unfireable, and for this fact the officials simply booted him, leaving the parents of the girl to press charges if they liked. Since there was no one to corroborate Stephen's side of the story, they took no action against the girl. The parents filed a restraining order against Stephen.

The police who delivered the order to our apartment advised me simply to get him out of town.

Stephen is fourteen, proud, ashamed, sick at heart, angrier than ever. Since the incident he has been unofficially attending classes at the public high school. He hates the sudden attention from the community. The story has been in the papers. Either at the high school or roaming the streets, he is out all day and most of the night.

And he is wary of my new, desperate tactics of *welcoming* his gang into our apartment, walking directly into Stephen's smoke-filled bedroom to engage them in conversations, offering them snacks and sodas. Their contempt for me is as thick as the smoke. They watch as I open a few windows.

"The landlords," I shout over the rap playing on the boom box. "We could get busted."

They laugh. They see through my housing and feeding them, anything not to lose my boy. Still, after a few days of this, they do come over more frequently, spend some of their evenings here instead of in the streets. God knows what they're planning. But we seem to have made a kind of sick deal: They are willing to use me; I am willing to be used as long as I know where Stephen is.

For the occasion of Christmas Eve, I have dressed up. The table is laid with a pale green satin cloth, the Lenox china, silver napkin rings, candles. In the living room I have set on the coffee table a punch bowl, cheeses, crackers, shrimp and oysters, holiday napkins, poinsettia paper plates.

I welcome Teddy, Alex, Jason, their mothers. Two speak little English, but their boys interpret for them from Spanish. Our guests are likewise dressed up. The mothers are single, and tonight I learn that these are their youngest children, all *prodigals*, my mother would say, like Stephen.

Teddy's mother has been of help since she owns a police scanner. Many nights she has called to warn me of reports of arrests she has overheard—car thefts and busted drug deals in which our boys might be implicated.

Though Stephen is still not home, we sit down in front of the fire. Charles emerges, sets his gifts under the tree. If I could stop the story here, it might appear to offer some potential for change. Imagine the city pausing to look in our windows, observing mothers and sons around a fire, carols on the radio, everyone lingering longer than they'd planned, having one more drink, another cake.

And assume that because of this stumble in time, some footfall on future disaster is averted. Such things happen: The delay in traffic means missing the collision head-on; a late airplane departure translates time and you arrive just *after* the bomb explodes.

Or maybe the delay isn't so monumental. Say it is only a minute or two inhabiting and inhabited by a little peace, a slight tripping of the dark. Maybe Teddy stays at our house later than he intends.

So he isn't on the scene when his gang sets fire to a car. He's late, he's simply not there, not for the arrest, nor for arraignment, the trial and sentencing. He isn't sent off to DYS for the rest of his adolescence. And after his release, more arrests, more sentences.

Nor will his friend Alex disappear, living child or body never found. We will never see Alex's face on posters around Brookline, later on milk cartons. What was waiting out there for Alex has left. He missed that bus.

Say something slides into civility.

When you can see a long way, you think it is the future.

I move to our windows above the street to see a small dark-clad figure walking up the hill, head down against the cold.

"Well, here comes Steve!" I interrupt the conversation. I'm a little mad these days, I know. My voice comes out of me shrill and too buoyant.

Stephen walks directly up the flights of stairs and into his room. In the wake of him the night air stirs the fire.

In a minute he appears at the end of the hall and signals his friends to join him. Sitting next to their mothers, Teddy, Alex, and Jason look at each other. I sense that they are enjoying the fire, the good food, this stab at pretending almost realized.

Then they get up and go to Stephen. Left in our ring, the adults are silent. Jason's and Alex's mothers begin to speak to each other in Spanish, gather their skirts around them and stand.

"I'll go see," says Charles, but he reappears pale, his face rigid. The mothers shout commands in Spanish to their sons down the hall. They nod to me and get their coats.

No telling what's coming, what's going on. But I am amazed that the boys obey their mothers. Teddy, Alex, and Jason appear outside Stephen's room. They are members of a gang. They steal cars, drive them around all night, then shove them off a cliff into a quarry. They run drugs, rob places, fight with knives, hurt some and plot to hurt others.

Tonight, obviously, there has been some kind of trouble outside, something that has caused Stephen to attempt to rally forces, but caught between the gang and their mothers, these boys choose, at least for now, the latter. They ready themselves to escort their mothers home.

I'm stricken with envy at this shred of respect.

"Merry Christmas!" I sing too loudly and head down to Stephen's room to find him unwrapping a gun, a real gun, maybe a forty-five, the bullets spilling out of the brown paper bag.

"It's not mine," he sneers, "in case you're wondering. Back off." Stephen waves the gun and grins at my fear. "I'm just keeping it for a friend . . ."

Before I can respond there's yet another knock on the front door. And at this moment—his first appearance of the evening—Stan comes up behind us. Surprised by his presence, I understand suddenly that he has been lurking, listening outside Stephen's bedroom.

"Give me that gun!" Stan swoops in on the brown bag and heads toward the door.

The gun's owner, a boy of about fifteen, waits in the entry. Behind him his own mother waits in the street, her car idling.

Stan bursts past the boy and heads out to the car. He leans down to the mother and exposes the gun.

"Your son just gave this gun to Stephen . . ." Stan is pale. "Take it now. Please take it out of our house."

But the mother speaks no English. She misunderstands. She thinks that Stan is pointing the gun at her. She speeds off, leaving her son, Stan, the gun, and now Stephen and me in the street.

Nine years later, I can't remember certain details of the evening. What happens to the kid? Soon the police arrive. They have been summoned by the mother from a pay phone at the corner of Beacon and Washington. At first the police intend to arrest Stanley for assault with a deadly weapon. Stan composes himself and explains.

As he speaks, the cops size him up. Stan's reading glasses hang around his neck, Bate's biography of Keats under his arm.

I think we end up again in our living room, the police, the kid, Stan, Stephen, and I. The cops take the gun, yes, but the kid vanishes from my recollection. Does he go with the police? Does he simply walk out the door?

And where is Charles in all of this? Among us? In his room? Not for the first, or the last, time, his brother's troubles eclipse him.

Then, when everyone leaves, the cops, the kid, I think we sit down to dinner.

Christmas Eve dinner, damn it.

And then Christmas day. We open gifts. Stan keeps the fire going. No one takes pictures.

And then we are relieved of the holiday.

Stephen flies with his brother to Missouri on the twenty-sixth "to celebrate the New Year." We are living inside pat cultural clichés these days, newspeak, huge warehouse phrases that are cold and empty.

The truth is that Stephen's father intends to keep him in Missouri. He will live there with his father and step-mother. Stephen's father and I have argued about the issue of how long Stephen will stay in Missouri. In the end he gives me an ultimatum: Steve goes to live with him for good. Or not at all.

Of course Stephen doesn't know this. He thinks he's going for a brief visit. If he knew the truth he would run away.

I watch him board the plane through the glass partitions at Logan Airport. I'm crippled by my betrayal, glad that his brother is with him.

Once the boys have boarded, Stan and I walk to his flight, boarding now, back to Maryland. We say good-bye. He hugs me, as is his way, firmly around my shoulders, kisses me. All gesture, all simple cultural convention. I don't ask why he's leaving early.

Alone in Brookline, I've gone to bed. I nearly sleepwalk through the teaching of my classes at the university, make short trips to the grocery for soup, bread, coffee. But the rest of the time I stay in bed with the electric blanket turned on high. It's February now. Stan stays on in Maryland. Charles is back at school, and Stephen is living with his father and stepmother in Missouri.

He's wreaking havoc on their household—sneaking out at night, inciting new friends to trouble—while I'm burrowed under, lost for a while, sad. I'm translating Dante.

I've accepted the assignment from an editor to take on the thirty-second canto of the *Inferno*, the Ninth Circle, Hell's basement, in which those who have betrayed family and culture are locked in ice.

So far I have written, *Were there a language dark enough to speak / truly of that hole harrowed by crags / gravity itself could not fall through to . . .*

The original begins with *S'io avessi—Had I*. Sinclair's translation begins *If I had*. But I take liberties. Just now I am more likely to side with those poor traitors stuck in the ice than with Dante.

For the past semester Public Enemy is what I've heard coming from Stephen's room, Public Enemy crowding me, crowding the spaces of this huge apartment while I wore headphones, the big kind that hug the entire ear. I listened to Beethoven's Opus 57, the *Appassionata* sonata, beginning to end. The little anthem with which the piece commences felt near to me even as the booming of open rebellion vibrated under my feet.

Stephen would have laughed, disgusted with me, if he knew what I listened to. He would judge me as irresponsible, an ostrich, pathetically middle class, a white chick wearing blinders—or in this case, earphones—against the social and political chaos he recently discovered in his young life.

Never mind my feeble offerings about growing up through the sixties, the marches I participated in, the protests. "I went barefoot," I heard myself absurdly reporting, "in winter. I hitchhiked. I had a boyfriend who quit school to protest the war. What do you want from me?"

Stephen wouldn't have it. "What about *now*," he'd say. "What are you doing *now*. Teaching at a cushy school full of white bread, writing poems nobody *gets* about *nature*. Listen up, Mom. Listen to these lyrics. Mom, you're getting *old*."

As the *Appassionata* moved up and down the octaves, great spaces built around me, as though days, weeks, even years had passed. Inside those spaces, my rage could rise and recede, leaving me stumped at how a vigilant daughter of the sixties could be accused by her fourteen-year-old son of social and political indifference.

I listened to Beethoven so many times that there were moments in the tape that garbled, went underwater. The music drowned. I listened driving to and from school, or driving around at night looking for Stephen, watching a weak sun rise over the abandoned train yards as Beethoven went crazy.

Beethoven. Public Enemy. I'm lying in bed imagining Dante looking through the language as through the wide-angle lens of a camera, framing, over the full range of the octaves, a dark place, a lake of ice unremittingly cruel.

It *must* be ice and not stone, not just because of the killing sensation of cold, but because of a fundamental belief humans hold in regard to ice. Ice cracks, it breaks up and thaws eventually.

No, says Dante. Not this ice:

Non fece al corso suo si grosso velo
di verno la Daniola in Osterlic,
ne Tanal la sotto il freddo cielo,
com'era quivi; che se Tambernic
vi fosse su caduto, o Pietrapana,
non avria pur dall'orlo fatto cric…

But even places on earth that have been frozen for thousands of years thaw finally, shift and thaw to reveal ancient surprises, mastodons, woolly mammoths. My oldest brother has a mastodon's tusk that I have seen and touched. I've petted the coarse hair above the ivory.

Ice cracks. It melts and offers, whole and preserved, sailors buried in permafrost along the Arctic islands. The flesh on their bodies is startling, intimate. The Arctic anthropologists are awed, silenced by their finds, by the sad flesh preserved, gifts of the ice.

During the autopsies performed by the doctors who have set up tents on the gray stony tundra in Arctic summer—the place so flat, so vast, one cannot tell where the earth ends and the sky begins—the exhumed's perfect, one-hundred-fifty-year-old faces are napkin-covered, as if to shield them from their own undoing.

Some of the sailors' descendants have been allowed to come along. Outside the tent, they finger the buttons on the jackets of their dead, the jackets and trousers and shoes that have been laid out in the Midnight Sun in the shapes of the men who wore them.

The buttons on the jackets are silver. One descendant asks, may he keep one? He's aware of a change in himself. He weeps without embarrassment before the camera. He says that to look into the face of his relative is to see his own, and his children.

Well, fine, Dante leers up at me a long watery grin through the ages. *That's "sweet." But the* ice *in Caina, Antenora? This ice will never, ever cric…*

I can translate about three lines of the canto at a time before I must take a break, slipping carefully down under the covers so as not to knock dictionaries, drafts, my copy of the *Inferno* from the bed.

Dozing, waking to translate a few more lines, I begin to

tire of Dante, his unequivocal ice, his righteousness, the way he goes carelessly over the lake kicking the heads riveted there.

No wonder they snarl at him. *Fuck him*, I think, and laugh at myself for the first time in weeks. I say it aloud. "Fuck Dante and his fucking *Inferno*."

My voice rings through the empty rooms.

During the last year with Stephen I'm afraid I have joined him in his foul mouth. It's something Stan has come to hate about me. Certainly, before all the trouble, I was a reasonable, benevolently manipulative post-sixties mom suggesting to my children that they "save the four-letter words for appropriate occasions. Otherwise," I'd coo, "they lose their power."

In the event that one or the other's judgments regarding "appropriate occasions" faltered, the boys were fined a nickel for the initial offense, a dime for the next, and so on, a sort of monetary Richter scale approach to the problem.

But when things began to slide with Stephen, he laughed at my solution, reached into his pockets, and tossed dollar bills at me. Where did the money come from?

"Appropriate occasion, Mom?" he sneered. "That's every fucking minute of my life."

From my bedroom I can look down the hall and into Stephen's room, exactly as he left it, on the wall facing me a huge poster of Malcolm X with the caption, "By Any Means Necessary," the only noise from there, his hamster on his wheel.

One evening as I'm working with the translation, eating something from a can, I realize that the wheel has gone silent. The animal Stephen has named for a famous surfer lies on the floor of his cage. The right side of his head is horribly swollen. He looks to struggle to right himself. I reach into the cage and try to set him on his feet but he falls to the side again and again.

Filling a syringe with a bit of water, sugar, and a codeine tablet, I hold the little flailing thing and inject the liquid into his mouth. After a few minutes he quiets.

I take him back to bed with me, place him on my chest, and lie back. When I wake he's dead.

I keep him with me awhile, examine him closely, sadly, the way one could never examine a body were it alive. I pry open his mouth to see the fine teeth, the tiny perfect tongue, his pouches full of food; he who was born, lived, and died in a cage, who meant little to his owner, this animal being a replacement for a previous beloved hamster named Fergie.

When that animal died, not unlike this one, of a massive swelling of the right eye—some sort of hemorrhage, perhaps—Stephen had grieved as intensely and openly as one would expect of this child.

So Fergie's death was surrounded by pomp and ritual, including a secret burial under a yew tree at the front of our apartment house—secret because the landlords forbid pets in the apartment. If they visited for any reason, we put Fergie's elaborate bright orange-and-yellow plastic Habitrail in the bathtub with the shower curtain drawn and the door closed.

Stephen even chose a tombstone, a piece of hand-sized black shale we'd brought back from Cornwall, and he wrote on the stone, in white-out, Fergie's name and death date.

Stephen had never attended a funeral, and so when I asked him to speak a few words over Fergie's grave—in a downpour, by the way, though we were protected under the huge yew—Stephen confused grief, as many of us do, with shame, and began confessing things—that he had smoked cigarettes, stolen money from my purse, that he had touched a girl on her breasts.

I doze again, dream in two languages . . . *per ch'oi mi volsi e vidimi davante / e sotto i piedi un lago gelo / avea di vetro e non d'acqua sembiante* . . . fall through the high drift, the cloud regions of the bells of medieval Italian to the jackhammer pounding of late-twentieth-century American English, the hamster on my chest.

Where do the guns come from?

I'm driving home, down from Portsmouth, Newbury-port. I've been looking for houses to rent, houses away from the city and its gangs and guns, but close enough for me to commute into work in Medford.

Where do they come from?

Stephen will be returning to me at the end of spring semester. He is in more trouble than ever. His father has thrown up his hands.

It's early April, a Sunday. Up from Providence. Nothing. Traffic, raining. Houses beat up, or the rent's too high. But I will find something. Sooner or later I will find a house for us.

In these few months while Stephen has been away, I've had a rest. I've slept, read, taken long walks in recovery. I've begun rigorous workouts at a gym. I am in training for my son's return.

As I've grown stronger, my fatigue and fear have given way to cautious engagement with the future. I understand now that no one has the answer to my son's troubles. My belief that answers come from others—from therapists, school counselors, or teachers, from the law—has paralyzed me. No one will rescue us. This is the way it is: Stephen's adolescence will feel like a lifetime, his fourteenth year like ten.

I drive east from Littleton, south from Salem, late in the day, snow on the ground in the lengthening light. Some days I allow myself a good loud blubbering cry, then take a deep breath, pull over, and fix my makeup.

Where do they come from, guns taken so easily into the hands of boys to be traded, lent, stolen, bought, and sold?

The boy Stephen loved toy guns. He collected an arsenal of toy machine guns, all olive-drab plastic, or camouflaged green, gray, and black. He wrapped the stocks with electrical tape. He, his cousins, and his friends wore army fatigues to look like the G.I. Joe figures they amassed, figures that come with tiny guns, knives, bayonets.

They played for hours, staging battles, building little forts in the dirt, creating front lines, and setting the tanks in staggered lines, contorting the soldiers in aggressive poses.

If they were lucky to have some fireworks—black cats or ladyfingers—they'd stand back from their combat zone and drop the fireworks into the bunkers.

Sometimes I was called out to witness the explosions.

"Mom! Come see! We're gonna drop the bombs now!"

I'd watch Stephen and his cousins touch the wicks of the ladyfingers with punks, as their fathers and uncles

taught them, then flip them skillfully toward the battle
scene. The little men went flying, the dust of the battles
kicked up, the pieces of twigs, grass, stones scattering that
were the bunkers, the boys by turns roaring with laughter
and admiring the smoke, how authentic it appeared in
miniature as it lingered over their destruction.

This was play and I recognized it as such. These were
boys playing army like my brothers used to, brothers now
educated, prosperous citizens with sons of their own—
sons who, summers, visiting the grandparents, played passionate games of army with my sons.

By the time we moved to Brookline, I was aware of the
culture's raised eyebrows regarding mothers who let their
sons play with toy guns. The neighbors frowned as Stephen and his friends, in full fatigues and armed with
plastic guns, moved down the sidewalk toward the park
to stage life-size battles.

I held my ground. This was play. And if the neighbors
didn't approve, they could read in the *Atlantic* in the autumn of 1989 an article by Bruno Bettleheim that gave
language to my instincts about toy gun play.

Bettleheim suggests that the phenomenon of young
boys playing with toy guns is both harmless and necessary.
They play with guns, he says, because they feel defensive.

A previous collection of essays in *The Uses of Enchant-
ment* discusses how children are perpetually bombarded
with feelings of powerlessness at the hands of the authority figures in their lives.

Against recent notions of eradicating violent fairy tales
from children's libraries, it is better, says Bettleheim, to
give them imaginary stand-ins with whom they can iden-

tify—for instance, the monsters and evil villains in the Greek myths or the Brothers Grimm.

Through their identification with the Cyclops, his brutal destruction of Odysseus' crew, children can imaginatively act out their anger at adults, their feelings of paralysis and despair.

At the same time, they can witness Odysseus' cunning as he plots the Cyclops' demise, moves his men, in sheepskins, out of the cave to freedom. Children can be both Cyclops and Odysseus, the evil aggressor and the heroic citizen who acts on behalf of others, slays the oppressor, and saves his crew.

Such stories, insists Bettleheim, instill little morality plays inside a child's mind. Rigorous and aggressive toy gun play is a form of such dramas.

But what about real guns? Does my son believe that to handle and trade them, to point one at a girl and threaten her is play? By allowing, even encouraging his childhood war games, did I inadvertently set him up for this confusion?

"It wasn't a real gun," he sneered the day he was expelled from the Park School for threatening the girl.

"But she *thought* it was," I argued.

"Well, she's stupid then."

Is it that Stephen wants, at all costs, to keep on playing, even though the world isn't playing anymore? Is he angry with the world for not playing? Is he using his own enduring belief in play to dupe and frighten? Perhaps he is angry with himself because he still wants to play and the world refuses. And why does the world refuse? Has it grown up and left Stephen?

I take exit 9 off the Mass Pike and drive the back roads toward Amherst. Some years ago I did a poetry reading there and I remember how lovely it was. I'm thinking about Bettleheim's ideas on what he calls an animistic or ego-centered imagination. Children, he argues, possess it. Everything to them is animated, alive.

Bettleheim insists that children cannot understand an abstract universe because such a universe is indifferent to them and this is too frightening to conceive. It enforces their fear that they are powerless.

Better to tell them, he says, that the world rests on the back of a benevolent tortoise than to try to explain the rotation of planets. Not until adolescence can they begin to grasp such abstract concepts.

Could it be, then, that Stephen has fallen into a well between a child's reality that everything is alive, and the encroaching adult view that it is not, or that some things are and some things are not? This is, and that isn't.

Is his anger partly a result, anger that has eroded his empathy and his ability to be loved?

Or has Stephen unwittingly replaced one game with another, replaced innocent play with dangerous play. Indeed, why does anyone give up one game for another? Perhaps because the first game has grown tiresome. And why has it grown tiresome? It has become predictable—one always loses at it. Or, on the other hand, one always wins.

In either case, it is no fun anymore. There is no sense of disappointment or reward. In fact, there results a sense of irritation, even anger at having wasted one's time in the first place.

What would make it fun again? If one can't change the outcome of always losing, or always winning, what could

DEBORAH DIGGES

be done to make the game challenging? Well, perhaps one might secretly change the rules.

I'm remembering now how once, flying to Denver, Stephen, Stan, and I played cards to pass the time. Not long into the game, we discovered that eight-year-old Stephen was cheating, hiding cards in his pockets or slipping them up his sleeves. We had offered to him that his cheating rendered the game no fun for Stan and me, to which, to our surprise, he had responded, "Guys, listen. There are no laws in the air . . ."

The prospect of playing Twenty-one bored Stephen. It was a game he usually lost at because it required him to practice arithmetic, the subject he most hated in school. So he had secretly changed the rules, changed them, at the expense of his opponents, to make the game fun for himself.

"You mean, 'It's not whether you win or lose but *where* you play the game'?" Stan laughed.

"Yep!" Stephen answered as he reshuffled the cards.

Route 9 winds north and west to Amherst, follows the trees, the stone fences, the small ponds frozen, holding the gray afternoon sky. How passionately Stephen played as a child. He used his whole joyful body as he became this or that character in a drama, as he dressed up as the young wizard Ged or, draped in blankets, crawled along the floor, tinfoil sword in hand, Odysseus leading his crew to safety.

And when did this play stop? It was the fall of 1988, the year Charles left for college. Stephen was just eleven. He and I rattled around in that huge apartment, the night and the cold crowding the many ceiling-high windows, everything there suddenly too big for us. Even to each other we seemed smaller, strained, self-conscious.

Our three lives had to that point so powerfully contained the others, and the loss of Charles—even in the face of our joy for his success, his new adventures—opened up bare rooms inside Stephen and me.

In an attempt to close the spaces, I'd rearranged the furniture in the apartment; into the corner of the kitchen moved a small table just big enough for two, laid out a bright tablecloth and a light left burning. Here Stephen and I ate together.

But the enormous rooms around us and the cold night outside bore through. Stephen would fall silent, speaking up only to ask if he could call Charles tonight. Of course. But Charles was often out.

So might so-and-so sleep over? But it was a weeknight, and though Stephen was certainly allowed to telephone, one, two, three friends in the area, the parents of the boys said no.

"How about if we curl up in my bed and I'll read to you?" I'd offer.

"I'm too old to be read to, Mom, remember?" was his reply.

"Awww," I tried to cajole him, "just one good story for old times' sake? *You* read to *me* now. You owe me fifty-two thousand and twenty-three stories. Read me 'For the One Who Set Out to Study Fear.' I love that one, don't you?"

"I don't feel like it, Mom. Sorry."

Indeed, about a month or so before, in the middle of *The Adventures of Huckleberry Finn*, Stephen had declared himself too old to be read to. But for years we had read to each other every night, sometimes for hours.

Though Stephen is exceptionally bright, perceptive,

taught himself to read at three, he possessed then and now a short attention span. At that time doctors, therapists, teachers rarely isolated the problem as attention deficit disorder.

And Stephen was much like his namesake, my youngest brother, Stephen, who had also been a very active, delightful, but challenging little boy. Stephen's behaviors were not unfamiliar to me. He was, to be sure, insatiable about his interests. Physically gifted, he spent the good part of any day on his feet. The one, perhaps the only meditative quality young Stephen possessed was that he was a rapt listener to good stories.

Stories were a way, for instance, to get Stephen to settle down enough to take a bath. Through the years we developed a repertoire of bathtub tales, most if not all focusing on the animals of my childhood.

Stephen's favorite concerned a little black dog named Vick. He loved to hear me tell how one day on a bike ride in the country, I heard puppies whining and barking somewhere nearby. Behind a farmhouse I found a mesh kennel full of small black dogs. When the owner came out of the barn and offered to sell me a pup, I was sorry to tell him, "I don't have any money. But I'd take good care of one . . ."

"You's a little Sugabaka, ain'cha? Live over to the apple orchard? Behind Main?" Stephen laughed at my overwrought affectation of a deep southern Missouri accent.

"Yes, sir," I answered.

"We-e-ll, telly what I'd do. I'd trade one o' them pups for a bushel of apples from your daddy's trees."

The tub stories were short, the length of the bath. Afterward, we'd settle in to read. And I began to see that by reading to him, Stephen's attention could be engaged for longer and longer periods of time. I hoped that eventually this experience would translate into other areas in which he might comfortably sit still.

Stephen leaned close to me, his head just below mine so that I could smell his hair, his sweet child's breath as now and then he asked a question or asked to be reread certain passages. As he became more proficient at reading, we would trade off, he reading one page, I another.

So we devoured fairy tales, myths, narrative poems, ghost stories, science fiction, and, as he grew older, novels. During art period and after school he liked to draw the characters we'd read about. Stephen pinned up his drawings until nearly every wall of his room was covered in pictures of Ged and the flying dragons from *The Wizard of Earthsea*, Long John Silver, Frog and Toad, Odysseus disguised as a sheep, the Hunchback of Notre Dame, the Cyclops, Cerberus, the Phantom of the Opera.

But the night Stephen decided no more stories, no more Huck Finn, he took down the drawings. He did so ritualistically, carefully removing the tacks and putting them in a box, piling the drawings, facedown, under his bed.

Against my attempts to rearrange our lives to minimize his brother's absence, it was as if Stephen decided to represent physically the emptiness he felt, and punish or deprive himself for the pain it caused.

"Be real," he'd mumble when I suggested how much fun the two of us could have.

"Well, we'll find a way. Honey, look at me. We'll be all right," I'd offer. That autumn an aspect of Stephen's character surfaced, as intensely dark as was the light we'd known him by.

"Stephen, you burn so bright!" we'd say when he was younger.

As an infant, Stephen smiled for the first time for his brother. But it wasn't just a smile. Stephen's face lit up in a wide grin. As Charles again and again brought his seven-year-old-face close to his three-week-old brother's, Stephen gurgled, struggled with laughter.

Stephen so captivated us that I forgot the tub water I was running for Charles. Not only did it spill over, but as Stephen smiled and shrieked, water poured down the stairs of our California condominium.

Eleven years later, as suddenly as that first brilliant smile, Stephen had gone dark. He behaved as if he were in mourning: for the loss of the brother who could make him wriggle with laughter, for the threeness of our family, and perhaps for what—as he moved into adolescence—he intuited as the end of childhood.

Even the clothes he chose to wear to school were dark—gray or black sweatshirts, black jeans. Day in, day out, his colorful skateboarding T-shirts, his bright jackets stayed in the drawer as he wore black, brown, black, gray, black.

What might help? How about someone besides Mom to talk to? A therapist named Mike. How about a new skateboard? In spite of the landlords' complaints, we actually built a four-foot-ramp for it in our living room. And how about trips to see his brother, his grandparents, his cousins? All of the above, none of the above, some—.

Through the autumn of 1988 there were fewer and fewer moments of closeness between Stephen and me. I felt like Chekhov's darling, Olga, whose obsessive doting on the boy Sasha pushed him further and further away.

"You must try to do your lessons well, darling. Obey your teachers."

"Oh leave me alone," Sasha said.

"Sa-a-sha!" she called after him....

Where do the guns come from, into the hands of boys like Stephen, boys who for reasons as various and unique as the boys themselves have fallen into that well between the living and the dead world, who have not yet made the leap, as others have, over the gulf, boys who are grieving, bored with the old games, who have been left behind, lost in grief, isolated and angry. And dangerous in their confusion.

"It's easy to get a gun," Stephen says to me over the phone several nights after my trip to Amherst. He knows his future has once again been placed in my hands. If I don't allow him back to Massachusetts, he may be sent to military school. Perhaps for this reason he is forthcoming.

"It's easy. Mom, listen. People just have 'em. The right people. Kids know who to go to."

"But where do *they* get them?" I ask.

"They case cars and houses and steal them. Mom, there are lots of guns out there. All kinds. Sometimes dealers send runners to states where the gun laws are easy. The runners buy the guns and drive them back. Kids have fake IDs that say they're old enough. Or they get them at gun shows. There was a gun show here last weekend. I could buy one in Missouri if I wanted. No problem."

"But don't parents find them? Doesn't somebody keep tabs? Don't the gun dealers double-check?"

"Mom. Get real. Where have you been? They don't care. They just want their money. Besides, if you get busted you just wait a little while. If you've got the money, you can always find someone who'll sell you another one."

When we hang up, I dial a realtor in Amherst. My conversation with Stephen incites the old panic, but I'm thinking hard. I'm beginning to piece together an idea. Maybe I can't stop Stephen's access to guns, not here in Boston, or Missouri, or Amherst. Nor can I take his grief away. But there might be something I can help him to do.

In my readings of late on children and criminal behavior, I've come across studies that show that kids who are cruel to animals are likely to grow up to commit murder. The statisticians explain that such children lack all empathy for other living things. They cannot identify with the pain they cause. It is likely they have been, themselves, severely abused. But not always. The clinical term for these children is attachment disorder.

Stephen's problem is different in kind, though the statistics are a clue for me. He has never been abused. On the contrary, much loved, perhaps even overly deferred to. He seems to suffer from *de*tachment disorder; i.e. the world is dying away from him, deanimating, but he still feels alive to it. He is mad at it because it won't play anymore, or offers to him the same old games, games he has outgrown and tired of. Still, what else is there? He is mad at himself for still wanting to play.

From my reading I remember that one way in which professionals report some success in treating children with attachment disorder is by supervising their care and training of animals. Children are put into direct and intense contact with one particular dog, or a particular horse. They are solely responsible for taking care of the animal's needs. They feed and water, walk and groom their animal, keep daily journals, discuss behaviors, progress.

I set up an appointment with the realtor for next Sunday regarding a particular house that caught my eye in my travels, hang up, and lie back in bed. Stephen once had such affection for his hamster Fergie. How he loved and fussed over the little animal. And then when Fergie died, Stephen was indifferent toward the replacement, poor little what's-his-name.

Stephen was afraid to love the second hamster because, as he had learned—just at the onset of adolescence, when the world had stopped playing, when the world had abandoned him who still wanted and needed to play—that with love comes loss, and with loss comes grief. Grief hurts. Some people give up to it, some fight it. Grief makes Stephen want to hurt back.

"It wasn't a real gun," he'd said.

"But she thought it was," I'd offered.

"Well, she's stupid then," was his reply.

Stephen's sadness belongs to him, and the way out of it. Much as all of us have tried, we cannot take it away. His sadness has stranded him. He is alone and can't cross over. But what if Stephen could feel empathy for something again? Maybe through empathy, he might find his way. Then and only then would his need subside, his need to taunt the world with a gun.

*My brother moves quickly, with purpose. He always seems
to have a piece of useful knowledge for those who will listen.
Strands of his long brown hair often fly with his words as
he explains something. Peering over the tortoiseshell frames
of his circular glasses at you, he checks to see how attentive
you are to his words.*

*I see no physical resemblance to myself when I look into
his face, but I know that my brother's eyes see things in a
similar perspective to my own. He needs to document moments—I through my camera and he through his writing
and painting.*

*Before he went to college, he used to paint in his room, all
night sometimes, images flying from his fingertips. By about
3:00 A.M. the paint would be thick in his hair, and whispers of
color smudged his cheeks and neck. He looked like an ancient
medicine man. The brush was his wand and remedy.*

He would often wear suits to school, in a ragged style

that was all his own—like they had been draped over him at the last minute before some important business meeting. Dabs of paint brightened the black pin-striped pants and ruined the businessman look. But that's exactly what he liked about it.

If he wasn't painting he'd be reading things like Karl Marx, James Joyce, or John Cheever, or looking at books about painting by David Hockney and Edward Hopper. On these days I learned the most.

When I came in from skating, he would invite me into his oil- and turpentine-scented room, the odor stinging my nostrils, caking a taste in my mouth. He would explain whatever it was that was registering in his brain at that time in a way that I was able to understand fully, simply because he has always understood me. Our blood runs deep like that.

Now that he is in college, his hair is wild, parted in the middle. A sleek ponytail mass hangs down to his shoulder blades. He's recently grown a goatee that gives him a Euro-look, a look that I never knew could exist inside our family's physical feature gene pool.

He and I are seven years apart, but a good history out-weighs any sort of awkwardness that might arise when we encounter each other now, along with the fact that he is my older brother.

Grade: D–
Mr. Digges, the assignment was a seven- to ten-page essay, including research, on a prominent American.

Portrait of Charles / Photo by Stephen Digges

Missouri. The late seventies. My mother, my five sisters and I walk together, shifting babies on our hips. We make our way along the fence to the one cherry tree in our apple orchard.

We pass the beehives, the rich summer foliage. On her walks, our mother has discovered that this year the tree has produced thousands of plump cherries. She wants us to pick as many as we can and take them home with us to make pies.

Our older children run out ahead to explore the barn. At this time my five sisters and I have eleven children—seven boys and four girls, in ages from about twelve to infancy. In the years to come there will be six more children born to the Sugarbaker women.

Because we have been to church, we are wearing dresses, pale yellow, blue, white. We know ourselves to be strong and attractive. There are ten years between the oldest sister, who is thirty-five, and the youngest, who is twenty-five.

In her late sixties, our mother looks years younger. She is among the tallest of us at five feet, ten inches. We are attentive to her now in ways we never imagined.

Our bare legs sweep the grasses as we shift babies on our hips or set them down to toddle along, our blond to light brown to chestnut hair combed back with our fingers, hair the color of our children's, our nieces and nephews. We are versions of one another, versions of the ancestors.

As we walk we compliment each other on how well we look, how Connie has lost weight after the birth of her Tom, how beautifully Rena has fixed her hair—many tiny braids swept up in a bun, and will she show us how it's done?

We have time before we put lunch on the table, and then all of us will be leaving, returning home with our husbands and children to Illinois, Florida, California, Washington, D.C., and Minnesota. Connie and her husband and two boys will drive home to St. Louis.

The fact of the cherries and whether they make it home with us is irrelevant. Our mother wants us to pick cherries together and we want her to have the pleasure of the memory. She'll write her sister about it, describe it in the evening to our father. Plastic bags in her hands, she is delighted, a bit breathless as she leads the way to the tree.

We have many questions for her and for each other regarding our children, their quirks and behaviors. Charles's teacher has expressed concern that he prefers to play alone rather than with the group, prefers reading to sports. Rena worries that her baby, Geneva, so named for our mother, doesn't yet sleep through the night.

Mother's concern is generous and devout. Listening to her advice we hear how cared for we were as children. Her tone is one we recognize and fall into. It is an aria, a fugue, a round that returns sympathy for discernment. We know it like birdsong, like water filling a sink, dishes as they are washed and stacked, and the smell of Jergens lotion.

"Charles is a thinker," she tells me, "like his grandfather. I see no problem with his playing alone, as long as he has friends."

"He does," I say. "Lots."

"Well, that's fine, then, darling. Remember your brother Paul—well you wouldn't. He's so much older than you, but as a little guy he, too, was quiet, loved playing alone and reading just like Charles. Sometimes I wept at how *good* he was. And look at him!"

Mother beams at the thought of her second son. "He's doing so well. Why he's chief of surgery now. And how he loves his daughters . . ."

"Charlie!" Mother calls my son from the group. "Will you pick some cherries for Grandma?"

"Sure," says nine-year-old Charles." He blushes and begins to pick cherries, eager to please his grandmother and happy to be singled out.

As he works, Mother points out the plumpest cherries to him and smooths his hair. "He's *fine*," she whispers and winks at me.

Now mothers ourselves, my sisters and I see her in a new light. We are beginning to understand her life as our mother, her enthusiasm and courage, her sacrifices. We are learning through her advice and care of our own children, and we dismiss what we once perceived as her injustices toward us. Indeed we agree that she acted in ways she believed to be best for us.

Telephoning long-distance, we say to each other, "How did Mom do it?" As we speak we remember our emotional, spirited, smart-mouthed selves, the six of us laughing, carrying on, playing at high volume the Beatles or Joan Baez in our suite at the opposite end of the hall from our parents' bedroom.

There we experimented with makeup—purple eye shadow, midnight blue eyeliner we'd bought against orders at Woolworth's, or we read aloud to each other from the romance comics we'd smuggled in.

Among our unmade beds, clothes thrown everywhere, empty soda bottles spoiling our antique dressers, the youngest were eager guinea pigs for the oldest, who permed our hair to frizz and once bleached mine pumpkin-orange.

Sometimes we talked disparagingly about our mother. "She's so old-fashioned," we'd say, "so *fundy*," we'd add, using a term we'd coined to describe the fundamentalist Christians at our church whom we judged to be hopelessly "out-of-it," overly religious people; "in la-la land!" we'd laugh.

"We should take her shopping," one of us would say.

"She's started to wear those ugly, loose, fundy dresses. And her hair!"

"*Some*one should talk her into coloring it."

"Maybe she'd be less strict with us!"

"Less out-of-it!"

And sure enough, after much thought and, as she would emphasize, "prayer," our mother, to please us, would submit to our ambitions, let us bring clothes we had picked out for her from the department store "home on approval."

Then in the afternoons when the youngest were down for naps, she tried them on for us as we nodded, marveled and fussed over her, or stood back and shook our heads.

Sooner or later she let us cut her long graying hair and color it with Clairol. She let us apply makeup to her face, pluck her eyebrows—"Not too much! Your father will have a fit!"—and touch her long eyelashes with brown mascara.

Sooner or later she allowed Gena a two-piece bathing suit. "No bikinis!" she called as Gena headed out the door to buy it. "And I have to see you in it *here*, before you go out of this house!"

Mother let me keep not just one but two stray dogs, let Connie and Beth cut their waist-long hair, let Rena wear a strapless formal, Eva the pearls my father had given my mother for the prom.

"How did she put up with us?" we ask each other, having just endured, ourselves, some minor crisis with one of our own children. As we say it, we know that the fact of her patience, her silence, her worry, her willingness to listen, and most of all, her passionate engagement with us will be the quality we must now emulate.

And so, like her, we become fierce mothers, mothers who plot and gauge, who measure and consider, who call one another for advice, reporting on a book or an article we've read, some insight we've had, each of us offering experiences in order to help our sisters.

Like our mother, we believe ourselves to be wholly capable. We exude an earnest, youthful confidence, a satisfaction as we tell one another how well this or that turned out—the birthday party, the camping trip, the teacher's conference, the math tutor, the bedtime problems.

Our children are the heroes and heroines of our narratives. We defer to them, to their intelligence, judgment, their abilities to adapt or stand up for themselves, and as we defer to them, we take pride in our direction.

We do not forget to tell one another, "You did just the right thing. That was smart! Good for you!" And we wait to hear such praise heaped upon ourselves.

We believe, as our mother, that we are doing it right, that we are good mothers doing the right things for our children. Perhaps we are even a bit smug about the ways in which our young children are prospering. Love is enough. Love is a compass that will show us true north. So we navigate by the stars.

We say to ourselves, "Of course!" when some crisis resolves. "Of course!" As we say it we hear our mother's voice piously quoting from the Old Testament, "Bring a child up in the way that he should go and in the end he will not depart from it."

In Brookline, many years from our walk to the cherry tree, things begin to go wrong with my Stephen. I talk to my mother and my sisters. As always they listen, consider, offer advice. Yes, they agree that maybe a private school is a good idea.

"Yes," my mother says. "You're doing the right thing."

But when the troubles exacerbate, when I begin to suspect drugs and guns, when Stephen's withdrawal becomes so profound he refuses to speak to me, eat at the same table, when he exhibits behavior I never imagined from one of my children, I call my mother and sisters less and less, then not at all.

My reports of Stephen's behavior have begun to shock them to silence. I hear their restraint. In their silence I believe that I am hearing their judgment of my son and me.

No, they have never experienced anything like this. How can they help? Would it help if they visited, or maybe I should send Stephen to them for a week or so. But in these offers I think that I detect caution in their voices, which I interpret as fear. I imagine them wondering how a visit from this wild nephew might affect their household.

"Don't worry—we'll figure it out. It'll be all right in the end," I say, thinking to let this cup pass from them. They continue to write and call, voice their support, and offer help, but I become evasive.

I am afraid. My identification with my son and my feelings of responsibility for his behavior are strong. I am ashamed.

How can I tell my good sisters, with their young sweet children, about the things Stephen is doing? Daily I navigate by shame that carries me far away from my son and my family. Surely any child who behaves this way has a mother who has done something wrong. What wrong? Something, something very wrong.

It's been years, anyway, since I've been home. I've lost touch with my family. I've been finishing graduate degrees, writing, divorcing, remarrying, moving my children with me across country, overseas to London, and back again. My life has taken a course different from my sisters'.

I battle guilt from my smugness, personal and cultural, that confuses and paralyzes me: in my mother's and sisters' eyes, certainly in my eyes, my son Charles has "turned out fine." That was my doing, wasn't it? He is a good young man now in his first year of college, an excellent student with friends he is proud to bring home, wonderful, polite boys who call me "Mrs. Digges," who carry my groceries from the car, open doors for me, boys whose company I thoroughly enjoy. This is because of my good mothering of Charles, right?

Then what about Stephen? Why is he so troubled? Why does he act out in this way? How can two sons of the same mother and father be so different? These are the questions that make me angry. I believe that Stephen is intentionally challenging me and I want him to stop. I want all this trouble to stop. I actually believe that he can stop it.

After all. Look at all I've done for him. Think of how when he was tiny I carried him everywhere against my heart in a Snugli. How many nights I rocked him through his colic, slept with him next to me, forwent school and sports events with his brother because he was sick, or fussy, or tired?

The time he was choking, just as he began to lose consciousness, I was the one who reached down his throat with my finger and pulled out that piece of a toy. And who built for him with my own hands skate ramps, read to him *every* night, coached his Little League team, who, who . . .

I hate hearing myself say these things, but I say them, as if to abdicate, to place the blame where it belongs. I detest this vision of myself. I tell myself viciously that I am a walking cliché of the bad mother, a bad mother, bad mother. I am brutal with myself and a shrew to Stephen.

I am someone I never imagined, an isolated, bitter, defensive mother navigating by shame the deep waters of her son's adolescence, a changeling so different from the woman with a baby on her hip, walking with her mother and sisters, older son, nieces, and nephews to fill bags full of cherries, bags that will be left in rental cars, in airports, or actually carried home, pitted, and made into a pie.

Cherry juice stains the dress she will travel in, stains that, laughing, she shows to her sisters as the children hold up their hands, sticky with cherry juice and the rich sap from the tree. Carrying her Stephen, she is capable, happy. She is a good mother, like her sisters a fierce mother, and her children will therefore be good, smart, educated, caring, successful—better people, no doubt, than she.

The first week of the ninth grade in Amherst, Stephen is once again in trouble. Stan and I get the call around eleven on a Friday evening. We've been preparing to get in the car to go and look for Stephen, who was supposed to be home by ten. We've been lingering in the kitchen, hoping he might walk in.

Stan's tired. He arrived in Amherst about dinnertime, having driven up from Maryland for the weekend.

"Guess what." He shakes his head as he hangs up the phone. "We *ought* to let him sit out the night in jail." Stan picks up his car keys and heads out the door.

Alone in the house for a few minutes I'm dizzy with disappointment. How can this be? I slide down the wall and put my head in my hands, thinking, searching the screens inside my head for an image, a mooring. When the car pulls in the driveway, I brace myself.

The scene that is about to take place is predictable. I

detest its familiarity, Stephen stonewalling Stan and me, me following Stephen up to his room, pleading, trying to make contact, Stephen turning with accusations and profanity. Then Stan, thinking to come to my rescue, getting between us, insisting, "You can't talk to your mother this way!"

In this tiresome drama, how well we know our parts.

Tonight there is one notable exception.

As a rigid Stephen, rubbing his recently cuffed wrists, walks in the door, G.Q., our new English bulldog puppy, runs right over to him, jumps up on his leg, and wriggles and whines with happiness, G.Q., who couldn't care less about the events of the evening, about open and sealed records, lawyers, court dates.

The puppy's joy interrupts the well-worn script we are each ready to play out. G. is so excited to see Stephen that he relents, stops the rubbing of his wrists and picks up the dog. We can't help but drop our guard a bit in surprise.

"Still—" Stan's heavy brows are knit frighteningly. "We've got to deal with this."

But G.Q. is licking Stephen's face, slobbering with joy. Stephen tries to stifle a grin. Holding the dog close to his chest he steers him—as a weapon, it might appear, or a shield. He turns his head from side to side, trying to avoid G.'s enormous wet tongue. Stephen and his dog make their way between Stan and me and head up to Stephen's room.

"Follow him," Stan urges, his voice tinged with helplessness.

"Wait," I say. "Let it go for tonight."

"But we've got to deal with this! We've got to deal with it *now*. He's out of control."

While Stan is yet excited, focused, intense, I feel an unstoppable draining of energy. Stan is trying to do the right thing, the way he knows, the way we know, though it fails us over and over.

We believe that to do the right thing means to confront Stephen, make him understand what he's done wrong, and then resolve this episode as best we can.

Then we must try like hell to regain our control.

Control, yes, this is the modus operandi. We must regain control of this kid, where he goes, who he talks to, with whom, for how long, etc.

We've already taken sanctions toward this end.

Every night at ten o'clock Stephen must unplug the phone extension in his room and deliver it to us. This particular sanction was enacted when, getting up to let the puppy out one night about 3:00 A.M., I heard Stephen talking and laughing.

Not only had he been on the phone all night, but when we received our first phone bill, it was clear Stephen was running up huge long-distance charges.

We took control by putting a long-distance block on the line, demanding that Stephen unplug the phone in his room and deliver it to us every night at ten. Then we grounded Stephen for two weeks during which the three of us drove around the New England countryside, Stan and I ogling the scenery, Stephen in the backseat, his eyes closed, his Walkman leaking a hiss and rumble as he listened to rap.

But soon we would learn that we had overlooked a few

details regarding the phone. As they came to our attention, we corrected them too.

We'd overlooked the fact that Stephen could—and did—borrow a substitute phone. Returning the official phone to us each night, he went back to his room, rooted out the contraband phone from its hiding place and plugged it in.

And though we had put a block against outgoing long-distance calls—except when using a special numerical code that Stan and I, like spies, memorized and repeated back to each other in our locked car, promising never, ever to write the code down or breathe word of it, or dial it in Stephen's presence—we'd failed to block long-distance calls coming *in*.

"That's a different *kind* of block," the AT&T operator explained to us. "It's not included with a direct-dial block. They're two different blocks, each with a separate fee that will appear on your phone bill."

"If I were to choose one," she continued, warming up to us when we didn't argue with her about the two fees, "I'd choose the collect-call block. Collect calls are more expensive than direct-dial, you know. *Much* more expensive."

"We know," we answered, Stan on the downstairs extension, I on the upstairs. "We'll take both."

"So much for the honor system," said Stan over the dead line, quoting the method of choice suggested to us by Stephen's former therapist.

"Ha!" I punctuated as we hung up and met in the kitchen for celebratory drinks.

But tonight we've lost our humor as we stand in the

kitchen racking our brains for a course of action, "That will get this kid in line," I say.

"And keep him there." Stan finishes my sentence.

In light of the last few years, the recent phone scam, and the events of this night, we feel that we have every right to forgo Dr. Mike's advice of putting Stephen on the honor system.

At this moment we both debunk all the child psychology nonsense we've been feeding on: the Erikson, even the Bettleheim, as we remember grueling, interminable therapy sessions we've sat through—a mute, sullen teenager on one hand and a pompous Dr. So-and-so on the other. We remember our hope following these sessions, how each time that hope set us up for disappointment.

"I read a piece in the *Times* the other day," Stan interrupts our silence. "It was about a father whose teenage daughter kept sneaking out to do drugs. Then she'd come home sick or out of it. She wouldn't go to school. One night she overdosed and he rushed her to the hospital.

"The hospital staff and the police gave her a choice of rehabilitation or jail. She chose the former. While she was away the father prowled the streets at night looking for the dealer."

"Did he get him?" I ask.

"No luck," Stan continues. "But before the girl came home from the hospital he installed more locks, nailed her window shut, and put up bars."

"There you go."

"Wait—her first night home from rehab she wanted to go out. Said she was going and no one could stop her. The father got out some chains and a padlock he'd recently purchased and had been keeping in his closet. He chained the girl to the stove."

"How?" I ask. "Where did he chain her?"

"Her ankles, I think."

"Like hobbling a horse," I offer.

"Yes, and then, I guess, to the stove. Then he moved her bed into the kitchen, all her books and school materials. The chain was long enough that she could move about pretty freely. She could even take a shower," Stan adds, as if to hold up the father's excellent calculations of the length of the chain in deference to his daughter's needs.

Stan watches as I imagine the scene—a girl dragging her chains into a shower stall, turning on the faucets. A girl in chains cooking supper, reading a book, doing math, or writing a paper. In chains, yes. Doing drugs. No.

"Did it work?" I say.

"He kept her from going out for more than a week. But one day he forgot to unplug the phone and put it out of reach and she called the police."

"Rats," I say. "Busted." We look at each other, then gaze, baffled, out into the dark.

We are no longer surprised with ourselves for our mutual consent to behaviors such as the father's, or of any parents we hear of whose desperate attempts at control are meant to keep their children from harm.

As we linger in our new kitchen, I'm noticing how thin Stan has become, his shirt and shorts loosely fitting his frame. Who could have told us, when we married seven years ago, that our lives would descend into this hell otherwise known as Stephen's adolescence, into one crisis after another with this child, at first just little things, complaints now and then from his teachers, his grades dropping in one subject, then another, then another.

Then the move to the Park School, where at first he appeared to apply himself, renew his hope and pride in things as we renewed our hopes in him and in ourselves as parents, only to have them dashed as street gangs infiltrated our world, as charges were brought against him, restraining orders brought to our door, cops to our door, guns.

When Stephen's own terror took hold of him now and again, when he wept in despair in our arms—just when we thought he might turn around now—he'd run away, disappear, come home, weep, threaten suicide, run again.

Sweeping his hand through his hair, Stan leans against the sink. We can hear the cicadas in the back trees as the late September night smells drift in the kitchen—wet wood and the first downed leaves.

Something in Stan has given up. I know it beyond my own dim sadness. As we move through the house now, shutting doors and turning off the lights, I try to remember the last time Stan woke me in the middle of the night to read me a poem he had just written, or I woke him to read a passage I'd just found in Keats's letters, or a passage from Hopkins or Akhmatova.

What had we thought, anyway? What had we believed our lives would be like after our marriage? I suspect we thought, like many parents, that my sons would grow up under our enlightened care and everything would be fine.

We believed that our parenting was superior, that we were, without a doubt, better parents than our own had been to us. We'd vowed not to make the mistakes they did, mistakes we often picked out and highlighted and discussed so rationally.

And we believed that our lives as writers, lives punctuated by travel, by liberal, ecumenical notions of culture and society, by our moves to this or that university to teach, by our stays in Europe, the boys attending school there—that all these experiences would have positive effects on our children.

Though Stephen's behaviors were hard on everyone, what was hardest on Stan and me these days was the fact that rationale and reason seemed trivial now, dizzyingly earnest. Our once sacred belief in the honor system had become a joke. Now, instead of judging our parents, certainly culture at large, for old-fashioned—indeed we'd often called them cruel—approaches to child rearing, we were looking to those approaches for answers.

Neither of us raised an eyebrow when one or the other fell into the doomed cadences of *that's the way my parents did it…*

As recently as two years ago Stan would likely not have paid much attention to the article in the *Times*, or if he had, he would have noticed it only to shake his head at what he thought to be a father's stupid brutality toward a daughter.

The quality I loved best about Stan was his benevolence, his stand against oppression. During the Vietnam War he'd been a conscientious objector. During our courting he had written me, *I'll do everything I can to be friend and father to your boys.*

I look down at my shabby T-shirt and jeans, my dirty

bare feet. Stan falls onto our bed fully clothed, sighs, and closes his eyes. He is used up by the first weeks of intense teaching and the commutes from Maryland to Massachusetts, where he is greeted by an anxious mother and an angry stepson.

"I'm sorry about this," I say as I lie down next to him.

"Sorry for what?" He stirs. "You didn't do anything."

"I know but—"

"But what. You were going to say, 'It's my kid.' "

"Uh-huh. Sorry," I say again, this time for making the distinction.

"Night," he sighs.

In the morning he wakes me with a note he has found from Stephen taped to the fridge. *I'm leaving for good*, it reads. *Don't try to find me.*

Stan is fully dressed. He has showered and put on fresh clothes. I see his backpack stuffed and ready at the foot of the bed.

"I can't do this anymore," he says as I sit up and shake myself fully awake. "I'm sorry."

Stan hands me a mug of coffee and smooths my hair.

"Take my advice and call the police and let them deal with him. When you do, let me know.

"And by the way," Stan adds as he readies to leave. "It seems Stephen took the dog with him, and a bag of dog food. And your car."

Stephen kissing G.Q.

We're dancing. The boys take turns being my partner as we dance to the spinet organ playing "Shine on Harvest Moon," and peppy versions of "Harbor Lights," "I'll Remember You," "Someone to Watch Over Me." Stephen likes to plant his little feet on mine—we sidestep the maze of cables, hobble and sway across the café's bright linoleum.

When thirteen-year-old Charles cuts in, he places his hand on my hip and concentrates on the floor. He has just outgrown me in height and we are startled by this new perspective that renders both of us a bit shy.

His height surprises us and sadly reminds me that just now we are separated, Charles living with his father in Columbia, Stephen and I in Iowa City.

I have to lean away from him because the brim of his Stetson keeps grazing my forehead. If I swing to the snare drum beat a little too enthusiastically, Charles looks panicked. So we step deliberately, meet each other's eyes, and smile.

This Friday night, like so many others, we planned to meet at our usual spot halfway between Columbia and Iowa City—the Bloomfield, Iowa, town square—so that Stephen could spend time with his father, and Charles with me.

But my Volkswagen threw a rod in Ottumwa, a town short of our destination. After calling a tow truck from a phone booth, calling Columbia regarding our situation, I carried six-year-old Stephen piggyback along the highway, our heads down against the November wind gusting off the fields on either side of us. We made our way toward the only establishment open now, toward the shuddering pink neon rainbow of the Stardust Lounge.

The boys' father occupies a table just off the dance floor. When we catch him looking at his watch again we wave. He throws us a resigned smile.

The evening our car breaks down in Ottumwa, it is the last night of the town's bowling league tournament. Teams are gathering at the Stardust Lounge for a celebration.

Sure enough, the boys' young stepmother, Terri, had relayed my message to Charles and his father. They'd waited nearly an hour in Bloomfield, then phoned to discover we were marooned in Ottumwa and came ahead.

We dance among five or six couples wearing bright satin team shirts of green, gold, and blue, their names sewn on the pockets. The boys are wearing oversized clothes they love from a secondhand store in Iowa City. Stephen's well-worn denim jacket has colorful patches sewn on the front—the Roadrunner, hot cars, and trucks. Though it's November, he wears surfer pants, and his favorite Michael Jackson tennis shoes.

Charles sports that Stetson, paint-stained jeans, a Hawaiian shirt, and an Iowa Hawkeyes tie, clothes he's not allowed to wear in Columbia, so he wears them to visit me.

I'm in jeans, boots, and a sweater. Their father is dressed impeccably.

We're odd among the bowlers in their team shirts and shoes, the waitresses in matching dresses and caps. The three of us appear to be out of uniform, or in the uniform of some tribe not native to these parts.

Before Charles and his father arrived, our waitress produced for Stephen a battered book of children's Bible stories, and between orders, she sat with Stephen explaining to him how Jesus loved him. Stephen was tolerant. He listened to her and nodded, though he tapped his little foot to the music. Perhaps to get away from her at last, he pulled me out on the dance floor.

So we're dancing. And when Charles and his father arrive, Charles and I dance, too. Soon Stan will be here to take Charles and me back to Iowa City while Stephen travels with his father to spend the weekend in Missouri.

My car will stay in Ottumwa until it's fixed.

We'll drive in opposite directions only to turn around and meet back in Bloomfield on Sunday night.

In the meantime we're dancing—Charles and I, Stephen and I, and sometimes, if we can convince Charles, all three of us take hands and create a circle, circle counter to the clockwork box step of the couples, the citizens of Ottumwa, my former husband looking at his watch, my future husband, Stan, who's just arrived.

The night's held back by our lights and the warmth of the café. Outside the window the extravagent yellow star atop its pink rainbow flickers and whines against the clatter of dishes and music. It washes our reflection, shows us luminously to one another.

We're dancing, our circle abutting the story in place, the couples moving against us, making room for us as we dance in and out of the margins. What do we know of our strangeness? So little yet. Exhilarated, feeling the pull of the centrifugal, we tighten our grasp.

Tuesday, 4:30 P.M.—Youths who had climbed the fire escape to the roofs of downtown office buildings and who were throwing objects at pedestrians were arrested and taken to the police station.

Saturday, 1:34 A.M.—Youths were reported to be skateboarding and causing a noise disturbance in the Jones Library parking lot. Subjects were gone when police arrived.

Sunday, 12:20 A.M.—A man reported to police that youths broke into a private swimming pool in Echo Hills and were skateboarding in the pool. Subjects were gone when police arrived.

Friday, 10:30 P.M.—Teens caught causing a woman to scream and setting off car alarms were sent on their way by police.

Saturday, 8:01 P.M.—Police removed fluorescent post-its with obscene messages from the walls of the Bangs Community Center.

Saturday, 9:45 P.M.—A woman reported to police that her daughter and some friends were harassed by youths making lewd comments and attempting to block the girls' paths as they were leaving the Hampshire Mall in Hadley. Subjects were gone when police arrived.

Sunday, 10:10 P.M.—Two girls reported seeing boys holding a gun while walking on Main Street. Police did not find the boys and couldn't determine if the gun was real or not.

Friday, 10:30 P.M.—Youths reported to be looking in car windows and trying doors outside Bertucci's were gone when police arrived.

Saturday, 9:30 P.M.—Youths fled police who confiscated a marijuana pipe and fireworks from the high school parking lot.

Monday, 7:18 A.M.—High school staff told police that someone had run a chair up the flagpole and painted obscenities on the wall leading into school. Police advised staff to question students.

Monday, 8:30 P.M.—A man told police that youths jumped out of the bushes at the corner of Amity and University and threw eggs at his daughter's car. Police are investigating.

Monday, 11:06 P.M.—A South Amherst woman reported that

her daughter was receiving annoying phone calls. Police referred family to the phone company.

Wednesday, 4:30 P.M.—Youths were reported to have released a pet snake among swimmers at Puffer's Pond. Subjects were gone when police arrived.

Friday, 11:43 P.M.—A woman reported to police that youths had thrown Slim Jims into her dogs' kennel and tried to coax them out. Subjects were gone when police arrived.

Sunday, 2:04 A.M.—Police found youths jumping from vehicle to vehicle on Fearing Street. No damage was caused by their activity, police said.

Tuesday, 9:30 P.M.—Police checked out speeding vehicles on South East Street.

Thursday, 2:19 A.M.—Police received a report that a person driving too fast on Hobart Lane left skid marks when leaving the area.

Monday, 5:20 P.M.—Amtrak officials told police that youths had jumped on the top of a passenger car while it boarded in Amherst and ridden to Springfield. Police are investigating.

Monday, 9:45 P.M.—Youths attempting to overturn an occupied phone booth were told by police to stop.

I am sitting in a waiting room of a therapist's office in tiny downtown Amherst. Stephen, who has been living at a friend's house, has agreed to meet me here. Yes, he'll bring the dog, too. Whether he comes home or not, he says he thinks I should take G.Q. home. He is worried about the pup, who is uncomfortable in a strange place.

What is in store is uncertain. I've spoken to the new therapist over the phone, briefed him on our troubles. The therapist has been recommended by the parents of the child with whom Stephen has been staying.

I imagine a session in which we'll cull the same grueling details of the last three years, details under which Stephen will smart and grow sullen; under which I, through the telling, will feel the old anger and frustrations rising.

The waiting room is lively—boys around Stephen's age

playing video games on the floor in front of me. From the room to my right I hear shouts and congratulations, Latin music from the room to my left.

I look around for something to read to isolate myself. They can't fool me, I'm thinking. I'm not about to get my hopes up only to have them dashed tonight, or tomorrow, or in a week—whenever tensions heat up between Stephen and me. Besides, it's 10:00 A.M. on a weekday. Shouldn't these kids be in school?

I hear Stephen and G.Q. approaching, hear the bulldog's panting, Stephen talking softly to him as they enter the suite. I spring up from my chair to hug my son, drop to my knees to caress G.Q., who is so excited he pees on the therapist's rug. Stephen takes a paper towel from his pocket and kneels beside me.

"He does this a lot," he says. "Now I come prepared. He's really missed you," he adds, blotting up the urine. "He hasn't been eating too well."

"I missed you both," I answer, trying to catch Stephen's eyes. "He looks okay. You've been taking good care of him."

When the therapist appears at his office door, we stand, stiffening again, freezing away from each other, the panting dog between us, stand up into familiar roles of difficult son and clueless mother.

But the dog won't let us for long. He's panting, huffing. Stephen breaks character as he suggests that maybe G.Q. needs some water. I fill the paper cup the therapist offers us.

The therapist gestures at the kids playing Nintendo. "Why don't you let these guys watch the dog and we go throw some knives and talk," Dr. Eduardo Bustamante greets us.

"Throw knives?" Stephen and I are baffled.

Dr. Bustamante doesn't look like the other therapists we've known. For one thing he is young—I imagine he is younger than I—and quite handsome. He speaks with a slight Spanish accent.

"Ya, throw knives—not *at* anyone." Eduardo laughs. "Well, not really. Come on in here, I'll show you." Eduardo leads us to the room from which I'd heard shouting.

"See you later, Isaiah," he says to a boy putting on his coat. "Here's the keys." Ed hands car keys and a ten-dollar bill to the kid. "I'll take the Super Chicken Burrito and a milk. You get what you want."

"Sure, Ed." The kid grins.

"Don't steal *this* car." Ed laughs as the boy heads out the door. "Little joke between me and Isaiah," he says to us. "Ever stolen a car, Steve?"

"No," Steve answers.

"Well, I mighta been known to," Ed says, laughing.

Ed offers Stephen and me a box open to knives of different sizes and lengths.

"These are just throwing knives," he reassures me. "See?" He runs his index finger against the blade. "Dull. Now, what you do is choose a knife."

Stephen and I look at each other. "Don't worry," says Ed. "It's fun. Go ahead. Choose a knife. Good." Ed beams as Stephen and I select a knife. "Now, throw the knife at the box."

Stephen and I look down to the end of the room to an enormous cardboard box—maybe a refrigerator or piano box—with crude faces like a lineup drawn with a marker across the top.

"Why?" asks Stephen, suspicious of being made a fool of.

"Because it's fun," says Ed. "Because you can get real good at it, use your lizard brain."

"Lizard brain?" I ask. I'm thinking that we need to get out of here. We won't be rude, but in a moment I will say that we have to go. We'll get the dog and proceed out the suite door and down the corridor . . .

"Never mind," says Ed. "We'll talk about that later. Steve, throw the knife. Let's see what you can do."

Stephen self-consciously aims and throws. His knife hits the board bluntly and falls clanging to the floor. Stephen folds his arms.

"Not bad," Ed comments. "First time and all." Ed fires a knife into the cardboard.

"Love that sound," he says. "You know that *thwak-tssst* . . . try again." He offers Stephen another knife from the box. Stephen makes another attempt.

"Now you," Ed says to me.

"Oh, I can't," I say.

"Go on, try, Mom," Stephen says.

"You guys keep practicing," Ed offers. "I've got to make a phone call. Be right back."

"But what about our session?" I say. "I mean, shouldn't we talk?"

"Sure, what do you want to talk about?"

"Well, this recent trouble . . . our lives . . ."

"Okay, if you want to. Steve, you want to talk about the past?"

"Not really." Stephen breaks into a grin.

"You know," Ed considers, "neither do I. The past is the past, right?"

"Maybe we need to be going," I say. "Stephen should be in school now . . ."

"Whatever you like. But why don't you throw some knives first. I'll just be a minute."

"We'll wait," Stephen answers for us. He would do anything to keep from having to go back to school.

"Good." Ed pats Stephen on the shoulder. "Good man. Help your mother," he adds.

"This is crazy," I whisper to Stephen when Ed leaves us alone.

"I know!" Stephen laughs, his face opening a bit, his eyes tentative.

"Crazy!" I repeat, grinning.

"I know!"

"We agree on that, do we?"

"Maybe."

"What are we doing here?"

"Dunno."

"In Amherst, Massachusetts . . ."

"Dunno."

"With our dog . . ."

"With our dog named G.Q. . . ."

"In the middle of the schoolday . . ."

"In the middle of math class . . ."

"Next to the fire station . . ."

"While the dog pees on the floor . . ."

"And you clean it up . . ."

"Because I'm used to it . . ."

"And carry paper towels in your pocket . . ."

"With kids playing Nintendo . . ."

"Instead of going to school . . ."

"And taking this guy's car to buy lunch . . ."

"We're assuming he's a car thief?"

"We're assuming they *both* are?"

"He said, 'Don't steal *this* car'!"

Now we're doubled over in laughter.

"And throwing knives . . . ," I say, hardly able to talk.

"Knives!"

"Yes, knives!"

"Using our lizard brains."

"Our lizard brains?"

"Our lizard brains!" Stephen stands poised. Between bouts of laughter, he aims and throws. "Here, lizzy, lizzy, lizzy!" he shouts. The knife hits the box and goes all the way through.

"Throw it, Mom!"

"Me?"

"Yes, you! Throw it! Keep your eye on the target. Okay! Ready! Aim! Throw!"

Mike's rise to the number one or top-ranking position in the chimpanzee community was both interesting and spectacular.... Mike had ranked almost at the bottom in the adult male dominance hierarchy. He had been last to gain access to bananas, and had been threatened and actually attacked by almost every other adult male. At one time he had appeared almost bald from losing so many handfuls of hair during aggressive incidents with his fellow apes....

All at once Mike calmly walked over to our tent and took hold of an empty kerosene can by the handle. Then he picked up a second can and, walking upright, returned to the place where he had been sitting. Armed with his two cans Mike continued to stare toward the other males. After a few minutes he began to rock from side to side.... Gradually he rocked more vigorously, his hair began to slowly stand erect, and then, softly at first, he began a series of pant-hoots. As he called, Mike got to his feet and suddenly he was off, charging toward the group of males, hitting the two cans ahead of him. The cans, together with Mike's crescendo of hooting made the most appalling racket; no wonder the erstwhile peaceful males rushed out of the way....

Eventually Mike's use of kerosene cans became dangerous—he learned to hurl them ahead of him at the close of a charge.... We decided to remove all the cans, and went through a nightmare period while Mike tried to drag about all manner of other objects. Once he got hold of Hugo's tripod... and once he managed to grab and pull down a large cupboard.... The noise and trail of destruction was unbelievable. Finally, however, we managed to dig things into the ground or hide them away, and like his companions, Mike had to resort to branches and rocks.

By that time, however, his top-ranking status was assured....

School photo

To walk into our house this morning is to enter a war zone. The awful aluminum doors have been kicked in. They hang from their hinges, the scalloped frames busted out, gouging the torn screens. The doors below the sink are likewise kicked in, and the door leading to the basement. Here and there is evidence of Stephen's attempts to assuage the damage, attempts at what Ed calls "reparation." Broken glass and Grape-Nuts have been swept into a milky pile. A brick props a cabinet partially torn from the wall.

It's spring in Massachusetts. Stephen is God knows where. Sometime in the night the car screeched out of the driveway and I understood that Stephen, his license suspended, must have secretly had a key made. Or maybe he hot-wired the car.

Our initial work with Ed seemed to create an iota of harmony between us, but the months since have proven that the problems we face, separately and in relationship

to each other, are no easy fix. With Stan gone—no weekend visits, no calls to either of us—I suspect that Stephen
feels a great deal like I do, hurt, confused, and abandoned.

And I imagine that from Stephen's point of view, he
feels suddenly stuck, locked in this life with his mother.
Apparently not the old scared mother, either, whom he
could easily manipulate, but some emerging animal of a
mother who attends parent-training sessions where she
learns "techniques" like refusing to listen to him until
he lowers his voice, playing dumb a lot to trick him into
solving his own problems, and walking away when he
kicks out a door. He is locked in with this infuriating
mother and the only thing to do is up the ante.

But what *is* the ante, and why must it go up? Ed warns
against it, but I still cull the past looking for reasons, in
the end unable to come to terms with Ed's idea that for
some children, indeed for Stephen, adolescence is simply a
nightmare, a terrible, seemingly unending nightmare in
which he is at risk, at one moment being chased down, in
the next doing the chasing. He is paranoid, besieged, his
hormones are raging. He is truant, destructive. I'm afraid
he will kill himself or someone else with that car.

And there has been another incident at school involv-
ing a gun. Granted, it was not Stephen but a friend of his
who brought it onto school grounds. The gun was brandished at a group of kids "in fun," Stephen explained to
the principal as we sat with police in the office. Who had
pointed the gun? Stephen refused to give names. Had
Stephen taken possession of the gun? He insisted no. He
only held it for a moment.

During the interview Stephen remained calm; the
mess in the kitchen is the aftermath of his rage at police

and school officials, and at me for attempting to question him further about the affair. He is suspended from school pending more investigation. In the meantime his license has been revoked for too many speeding tickets.

Driving through town one evening, I was pulled over by the police. When the cop came to my window he apologized.

"Whoops!" he said. "I thought you were Steve. I know the car, you see . . ."

The car, the car, the car. The gun, the car, the gun, the car. Where is Stephen at this moment? What speeds did he drive to get there? I'm remembering along Route 2 the makeshift shrine—a cross, some teddy bears—erected at the spot where a teen collided head-on, killing himself and the driver of the other car.

The car, the other car, the car, the tree, *he lost control of the car . . . trying to pass on a hill . . . a high-speed chase ending in disaster . . .* The car, by now full of dents, scrapes, hardly recognizable from just six months ago.

"Is that the same car?" a friend asked me recently. "Christ, it's taken a beating."

"What are you waiting for?" I ask myself. "What?"

"I hadn't figured on the car," I answer. "It hadn't occurred to me. I don't know why. I should have been more prepared. I should have anticipated this better . . ."

Looking out over the yard, the first green dusting the woods beyond the fence, I'm numb at the center. There are mothers rising this Saturday morning to fix breakfast for their children, or packing the car for some outing with them—a game, a hike, a shopping trip. These mothers do not jump every time they hear a siren.

And there are mothers who are preparing to drive to some prison or other to visit their sons, sons who have committed crimes that have landed them behind bars for a year, for five, for life.

There are mothers, too, who wake to a day that includes the knowledge of the death of one of their children, the knowledge simply of one of them gone, pictures around the house, memories, but the child—that one there—dead and gone. Was there any rescue possible, any postponement that might have derailed tragedy? No doubt they ask themselves this from time to time. And what advice might they have for me this morning? What would they tell me?

Moving through the kitchen, I head down the basement steps and open the storage room door. By the light of a weak bulb, among old mops and brooms, boxes of childhood toys and baby clothes saved through our many moves, I survey a steamer trunk I have secretly packed with new clothes for Stephen, soap, toothpaste, toothbrush, one pair of dress pants, one white shirt, and tie, the kind of trunk we might have packed once for summer camp.

Stephen's father has found a residential treatment center to which we plan, at last, to send Stephen. Of course, he would never agree to this solution. But the center we have in mind will actually send people, *heavies*, as I think of them, who come to town, then wait for the best opportunity to take him away—late at night or early in the morning. They spirit him away to the center where under close supervision he will go to school, work, attend therapy sessions, play mandatory team sports, etc.

If, after a year, he is *fit to reenter the community*—he'll be sent home. If not, he is *detained another year* . . . It's up to me to make the call.

Baba Yaga's house sits on chicken legs, walks by itself, and twirls around from time to time like a dancer. Baba Yaga does not welcome the initiate who has come to ask her help: The fire has gone out at home. Could she please borrow some fire? No, answers Baba Yaga, not until Vasalisa has completed a number of difficult tasks.

The story I read to Stephen many times when he was small comes back to me. Now, like Vasalisa, I'm at work in the first initiations, coming to grips with the fact that I must not look to Stephen to change, but to myself. The fire has gone out at home. Much is in question, here at the eleventh hour. I find myself relearning things. Under siege I forgot them.

Along with Stephen's troubles, my sense of failure at the prospect of a second divorce undid me for a while. I lost the way. Through last winter, as the dog and I maneuvered filthy, ice-crusted snow, I wept at the idea of myself as "a woman alone," as my own mother called it; a woman without a man in her life. Though I understood the irony, the fact that both of my marriages were to men who were for the most part absent, I hadn't grasped how tied I was to the idea of a husband. Moreover, the idea of myself as a married woman.

I suspect that I felt sanctified by culture. My grief at the end of my marriage to Stan translated as well as grief over the loss of that sense of sanctification.

By way of attempting now to drop this pretense, there are new things to consider. What are they? They are hard to name. They begin without language. Or they are imbibed with a privacy that refuses words. They seem to come from the same place my poetry does, as if all these years I'd sought to house each in different chambers in an attempt to keep my mothering separate from my art. Did I believe that one was more pure than another, that their morals were at odds? Was my work my wildness and my mothering its antidote?

What is Vasalisa learning? The first task demands that she let the memory of her own good mother die. She must stop looking for her mother's blessing. She is cleaning Baba Yaga's house, separating mildewed corn from good corn, poppy seed from dirt, dusting the bolts on the doors and shutters made of human fingers.

The steamer trunk so carefully packed for Stephen pending the event of his abduction to the residential treatment center sits gathering dust in the basement. Of his own accord Stephen has set the car keys aside and turned in his license. At a recent court appearance the judge told him unequivocally that were he caught again in the car, he would be arrested, charged, and sent to juvenile detention for no less than a year.

Coming in from Boston one evening, I find Stephen amidst bike parts in our garage. "I'm fixing it up," he says. "If I get caught driving I'm *fucked*." Without looking up at me he asks, "Do you want my keys?" He laughs. "I've got about six or seven sets hidden around here . . ."

"I've got keys," I answer. "But hey, it's good to know there are extra ones around."

As for the gun incident at school, he is excused of any crime, the dilemma of whether holding a gun constitutes possession decided in his favor. The grace of these two resolutions stuns us. We seem to want to hold on to the feeling, which renders us terribly polite to each other.

And now it's summer. We are relieved that school is out. We sleep in, we are lazy. Stephen stays up each night working in the darkroom we've created in the basement, or mixing music on his synthesizer. Friends come and go. I've taken to gardening. I like to work after the sun goes down, carrying candles and a thermos of iced tea into the dirt. I, too, work past midnight.

I'm thinking, digging, planting. If study is a kind of prayer, then I am praying. I begin to understand that there is no rescue after which we are returned to our old lives. Of all the expectations I've entertained, perhaps that one has been the most destructive. I'm thinking of Vasalisa's name. It sounds to me like *vacillation*.

One night I leave my gardening to go look up the word in the *OED*. Dirt smears the page where I read, "from the Latin, to sway, totter . . ." "I accept that," I say, returning to the garden, musing on the moment of the word, the slide and now of it. *Vasalisa, vacillation.* From the basement windows I can hear Stephen mix and remix phrases of music as he carefully dubs in each transition, backs up again and again to smooth out and resurface voice to instrument, voice to voice, instrument to voice.

Sometimes I'm invited down to Stephen's darkroom to watch by cave light the faces of friends and strangers, now and then my own, float to the surface of the page, take on definition, light and shadow.

"Wait till you see this one." Stephen stirs the water in the pan. "The bike's turned out to be a good thing for my pictures. I'm closer, I notice stuff . . ."

"Who's this one?"

"Watch . . ."

I begin to make out shapes, gray on gray rising, a pile of stones, tombstones? A rubble pile, I see now, behind a barn or shed. A rubble pile of tombstones shining in the watery residue. On each stone comes clear the word *Father.*

Things sway and totter. Much we simply let slide, much sits unfinished waiting for later or never—the gardens, the stone walks. There will be no man coming home at the end of the week, or at the end of two to point out all that should have been done, or redirect the doing—no one, in an attempt to father, to sneer at Stephen's hair or tell him to pull up his pants.

I know there are good marriages out there, good men and fathers, stepfathers. I know that Stephen's father and Stan had good intentions. But I begin to see how destructive the dynamic was and the expectations and disappointments it created. In this regard I consider my responsibilities and my complicity, my earnestness in trying to make it work.

I vacillate, finding my way into rapt relief that I don't have to be that woman anymore, no one's long-distance wife and lover attempting to make up for lost time, covering up flaws to make the weekend or the holiday *appear* as if all were well. Stephen and I no longer have this distraction.

There are dishes on the roof—Blue Willow—where we have taken our dinner, tools in the kitchen, birds' nests in the dining room, books waterlogged and swollen but not unreadable on the patio, half-finished drawings, wallpapering, remixes, half-swept floors, half-finished poems.

The house becomes roomy. It blurs with the outside. At night we prop the doors open for the breeze and fireflies float in. We switch off the lights and watch them. By morning there are many various and colorful moths clinging to our ceilings.

Father stones / Photo by Stephen Digges

One day on his bike Stephen finds a stray cat, tucks her in his jacket and brings her home to live with us. He names her Mugsie. A few weeks later she gives birth to a litter of kittens, four in all, which we end up keeping, every one. And when Charles goes to live and work in Russia, we agree to look after his San Francisco–born basset hound, one-year-old Rufus. And we adopt another bulldog, this one, as we know, with epilepsy.

A neighbor who has seen me walking G.Q. has told me about Buster. The dog was her brother's, but her brother has moved into Boston and cannot have pets where he lives.

Her brother gave Buster over to the care of a family in New Hampshire, but now that family can't cope with his epilepsy. About once a month, my neighbor explains, he has cluster seizures—one, two, three, as many as twelve over a twenty-four-hour period.

The family keeping the dog in New Hampshire has notified my neighbor's brother that it can't keep up with the dog's problems. The family has taken Buster to a veterinarian who recommends that he be put down. His epilepsy is severe, says the vet. Unless the family is willing to put in a great deal of time and effort, it might be better for the dog to be put out of his misery.

One Saturday in October, leaving Stephen in charge of Mugsie and her kittens, Rufus, and G.Q., I drive up to New Hampshire to meet Buster the bulldog.

I know little except what the New Hampshire woman has told me—that he is about four, that he is good with kids and other animals, that he takes a battery of medications each day on a precise schedule, medications the New Hampshire family will gladly give me for free if I take the dog off their hands.

"He loves to play with balls," she adds.

As instructed, when I reach the city limits, I stop at the 7-Eleven and call the number she has given me.

"I'm here," I say to the woman who answers. "If you could give me directions to your house now . . ."

"Just wait there," the woman says. "We'll bring the dog to you."

This is odd, I think as I hang up. I am a bit nervous about adopting this dog with epilepsy, sight unseen, from people who don't want me to know where they live, who know nothing about me, and who are so desperate to get rid of him, they'll hand the dog over to me at an interstate 7-Eleven. Were I to consult Stan at this moment, he'd explode, *What are you thinking?*

But these days, Stephen and I are more and more in-different to conventional modes of behavior. We're taking risks together for the first time in years, and in so doing we seem to be breaking free of the rigidity and fear that for so long dictated.

Over the past year Eduardo has helped us. And when the bills became so tremendous that it looked like we would have to stop therapy with him, Ed assigned me the task of editing his workbook, a book he would give parents and children regarding his often unorthodox approaches to troubled teens and culture.

We worked out a barter—my editing for sessions for Stephen and me. And through editorial reading of Ed's *Play and Pride*, I came to know his ideas and philosophies well.

Ed's office also became a refuge in the event of a dis-agreement. In the first months with Ed we discovered how easy it was to fall into the old patterns of rage and isolation.

"You need to practice detachment," Ed would say, tak-ing time out from a session he was conducting to look in on me. Having literally run up to his office, I sat weeping in the knife-throwing room.

"And go ahead and cry *here*." He patted my shoulder. "But when you go home, don't. Don't cry in front of Steve if you can help it."

"He's locked me out of the house." I hated hearing myself whine.

"We'll work on this," Ed reassured me. "We'll make it fair. For now, relax. Throw some knives, or play a little Nintendo. And when you're ready to go home, don't expect this kid's sympathy. Use your head. Climb in a window. Have humor. Practice detachment. And go in prepared to be effective."

Through Ed's guidance, counseling, and coaching, Stephen and I have come to understand our relationship almost entirely through fairness, through what's fair to each of us in any given situation. Fairness—or the lack of it—was at the root of most of our problems, and by extension, Stephen's problems with authority.

"You probably raised Steve with two goals in mind," Ed said to me one day. "You wanted to protect him, and educate him, right? I don't doubt that you've been a good mother."

"You're right," I'd said, tears coming to my eyes as I listened to him. "And thank you. You're the first person in a long time to say that."

"Wait." Eduardo smiled at me. "It gets better. You gave this kid a lot of freedom while he was growing up. I saw right away that Steve is the kid of a baby boomer, maybe the kid of a true child of the sixties. Come on." He laughed. "I bet that once you thought of yourself as a real flower child."

"Something like that," I answered laughing, letting the tears come freely.

"You really wanted things to be different for him—different than they were for you. I'll tell you, Steve has a very sophisticated vocabulary for his sexuality, for instance. He seems real at home in it, freethinking, comfortable. That was your doing, right?"

"I worked at it for both my boys," I said, blowing my nose.

"You really let them discover things without making a

lot of moral judgments, let them wear the clothes they wanted, play with toy guns. You let them make a mess, even take risks you thought might be a bit dangerous. Stephen tells me you let him build fires when he was little . . ."

"That's because he was obsessed with fire," I jumped in defensively. "I thought if I let him build—*campfires*, we called them—and oversaw it, let him explore his fascination in a safe context . . ."

"Did it work?"

"I think so . . ."

"See, you were right. You protected while you educated."

"That was *before*," I'd countered. "Think of our lives as *before* and *after*. Before was good. After is hell."

"It's hell because it's turned unfair," Ed answered. "Kids like Steve have come to understand themselves as capable, independent thinkers by the time they reach their teens. Despite their problems with impulse control, even problems with conventional learning, they believe in their abilities to solve their own problems because— Steve's an example—they've been allowed to. Or because—like his street friends—they've had to.

"After a childhood of being allowed to make his own decisions—after your encouraging him to explore his passions and play them out, even when they were a bit dangerous, even when they involved risk—*now* you're telling him no. That's all over. Now he's got to do what you say, what his teachers say, what the cops say, no questions asked."

"But the stakes are so much higher! He got himself into gangs and guns. And he's still just a kid. He's failing school . . ."

"Okay, okay. Listen. What do you want right now for *you* and Stephen?"

"I want us to be able to talk without screaming at each other, without his running away all the time. Breaking all the doors. He really has a thing about doors."

"Try joining him."

"Huh?"

"You've got a thing about doors yourself."

"What?"

"Come on. You've got a bit of an attitude yourself, Digges. I bet you've kicked a few doors yourself." Eduardo laughed.

"That was a long time ago."

"Too long. Look, this strict controlling parent thing you've been attempting is all wrong for you. Your heart's not in it. It's not what you do best as far as your parenting goes. Steve knows it. He thinks you're being phony."

"He's right."

"Let go of it, then. Join Steve. Join him in his anger at life. Join *him* when his teachers call him on the carpet for being late to school. Don't *educate* about what he should have done. Let him figure it out.

"And don't try to *protect* him from the consequences. Get out of his way. Hug him when the cops bring him home, hug him, and then shut up. Listen to what he's got to say. He *has* remorse, but when you jump in with questions and accusations, he turns it against you. Let him own it."

"But he can't be on the phone all night," I argued another day in a session with both Ed and with Stephen.

"If Stephen thinks he can be on the phone all night

and still get up for school, *and* pay his own phone bill, it's fair to say he should be able to do so," Ed had countered. "Right, Steve? Isn't that fair?"

"Sure," said Stephen.

"But what if he *can't* get up for school? Or pay the bill?" I said.

"Well," Ed considered. "What would happen to you, for instance, if you couldn't get up for work or pay your phone bills?"

"I'd lose my job," I said. "And they'd turn my phone off."

"Right."

"But school is different," I said.

"Well, not really. I mean for a kid, school is like a job. If Steve misses school, he gets fired, sort of. Then he can either try again or drop out for a while, then go back. Or maybe he won't ever go back. Right, Steve?"

"Right!"

"And were he to flunk out of school, it would be un-fair of him to expect you to support him. Nope," Ed spoke casually, "that would be unfair, and we've agreed, haven't we Steve, that it's important to be fair. No, it wouldn't be fair for you to support Steve, any more than it would be fair for him to have to support you if you lost your job. Steve wants to be independent, right, Steve?"

"Uh-huh."

"You want to be able to do what you want, when you want to. Right?"

"Uh-huh."

"Good man. Of course. We all do. We all want to be independent. So Steve would need to find his own place to live, get a job to support himself. In fact, look here, Steve. I saved the want-ads section of the paper for you. And here is a list of apartments."

Ed opened the paper and began reading descriptions of apartments aloud. "Here's one: 'one bedroom apartment in North Amherst.' Whoops," he interrupted himself. "If you live in North Amherst you'd need a car . . . can you get a car?"

"My license is suspended."

"Who needs a license? Weren't you by yourself when you were driving Ray's car the other night? You know, the night they picked you up . . ."

"Ya, but . . ."

"But you got caught, huh. Well. Maybe you couldn't depend on Ray's car every day. Or if you got caught again driving alone—what'd they say?"

"They said if it happened again, I go to juvie . . ."

"Bummer," Ed replied. "Geez! Those Amherst cops are rough. Wait! Here's one. It says, 'Apartment on bus route . . .' "

* * *

The concept of fairness is the method by which Stephen and I decided to adopt Buster the bulldog.

"I think he's going to need a lot of care," I'd said when I hung up the phone with the woman in New Hampshire.

"Like what?" Stephen asked.

"Well, she said medicate him every morning at seven. And he takes some other kind of medicine on his food, so he has to eat then, too. And we can't just feed him and not the other dogs. G.Q. and Rufus will have to eat then. Some mornings I've already left for Tufts by seven."

"We could take turns," Stephen suggested.

"But that's early for you. It's hard for you to get up and off to school. I'm not sure it would be fair to ask you to do that."

"They're probably going to kill him if we don't take him."

"True."

"And I'll be away now and then . . . I have some readings next term. One's in California. What if he's having seizures?"

"I could take care of him. Mom, listen. Let's do a trial. Let's say we'll try it with this dog. Two months. Let's say a two-month trial. In that time we'll learn what to do. We'll teach each other. If it's just too hard, we'll find him another home. I'm willing to try if you are."

"It's crazy," I said.

"Kinda."

"A third dog?"

"I know!"

"With epilepsy."

"Fits!"

"Fits, as in *Hey, kid, you're a step ahead of a fit!*"

"Named Buster."

"Who likes to play with balls."

"Get the ball, Buster!"

"Get it? Get the ball-buster!"

It's a cool, drizzly fall day and the 7-Eleven is busy as a car pulls up, the driver scanning the parking lot where I wait, a brindle bulldog hanging eagerly out the window. I wave and the woman stops her car and nearly runs to the passenger side. She leads Buster on a leash toward me.

"Are you Deborah?" she asks, thrusting the leash in my hand.

"This is Buster. Say hello, Buster! Now you hold him while I get his meds."

I kneel in front of the dog, his beautiful bulldog's face—not quite as flat as G.Q.'s—thrust into mine. He is also somewhat taller, a lighter golden brindle, more sleek, as if he might be part boxer. We smell each other. He licks my face as I hug him.

"Buster," I say. "Hello, Buster."

"Here." The woman hands me a plastic bag full of meds. "The instructions are on the bottles. A Valium in the morning at seven, and one at seven in the evening. Feed him twice a day at those times and put a capful of the potassium bromide on his food."

"Do you have his records? His shots and stuff?"

"I'll send them. Okay? I forgot them."

The woman bends briefly to pet Buster on the head. " 'Bye, Buster," she says. "She'll take good care of you."

Some years later, the morning following his death, while I'm digging Buster's grave, digging a deep, fine hole back near the woods in which I set down pictures of us, Buster's basketball, and a couple of Valium for the after-life, not without popping a few myself, I'll remember the day I met Buster the bulldog at a 7-Eleven in New Hamp-shire, and fell in love.

As I struggle against tree roots, the mossy black soil, I'm thinking how from the day I brought him home to Amherst Stephen and I came to love this dog.

We loved him ridiculously, without self-consciousness, as did the other dogs and cats of our household. Our cats came to greet Buster as they greeted us, rubbing against him and purring. They curled up next to him on my bed. After a while Rufus and G.Q. allowed such greetings and sleeping arrangements since Buster had shown them the way.

"He's our Vergil," Stephen once said.

During his seizures we learned to hold him while he frothed at the mouth, lost control of his bladder and his bowels. And then, covered in slobber, urine, and feces, we helped him to his feet as he recovered, praising him, offering him meds in a hot dog, the water he so badly needed after an episode, washing him down with warm towels before we washed ourselves.

Often Buster would begin a cluster of seizures during the night. I'd be awakened as the bed in which both of us slept began to vibrate, Buster rigid, rising toward something, his eyes fixed on the ceiling as if someone were calling his name, or he envisioned a ball being held up just out of his grasp. Then he would fall into a seizure, flailing, arcing his back as he rolled and wheezed and panted.

Stephen, who at 3:00 A.M. might well be in the shower or cutting his hair, would hear the commotion and know to run down to the kitchen to get the Valium. Then, as I lifted the dog to the floor to clean him up, Stephen stripped the bed and changed the sheets.

Once Buster wandered through our gate and was lost for an afternoon. Banking on the basset hound Rufus's strong sense of scent, we instructed him, "Find Buster, Rufus!" and Rufus had pulled us with authority on leash through the backyards of Amherst, but, as it turned out, in the opposite direction.

Buster had wandered down to the retirement home a few blocks from us. There he was befriended by the residents and the nursing staff, who let him wander about the halls while they called the police.

"I'm so relieved he's safe," I said to the nurse leading

me to the dayroom where Buster sat eating potato chips fed to him by a man in a wheelchair.

"He has epilepsy," I told her.

"Well, honey, don't worry," the nurse responded as she knelt to pet Buster. "He's come to the right place."

If Eduardo instilled in us the idea of fairness, then Buster gave us the opportunity to practice through our shared responsibility of his care. His condition demanded discipline—we *must* get him fed and medicated by seven or by mid-morning he would be seizing.

And when seizing, he couldn't be left alone. Someone needed to be with him. Often the local vet kept an eye on him the days I drove into the university. Like the retirement home staff, the clinic allowed Buster the run of the office. After school it would be Stephen's job, rain or shine, to go to the vet's and walk Buster home, have him fed and medicated as well as feeding Rufus, and G.Q., and the cats, by the time I walked in the door at seven.

Because a ride in the car calmed a seizing Buster, I sometimes took him in to Medford with me, stopping at rest areas to let him pee, wandering around the area a bit with him so he could stretch his legs and explore, then loading him back in the car. Were this the case, I needed to leave an hour or so earlier than usual. His needs insisted that we plan our days; at the same time we must be willing to depart from our plans.

Maybe Stephen promised friends he'd hang out after school. Maybe I was tired and could have used an extra hour's sleep. Or maybe I was working on a poem. Things must be put aside in deference to Buster. Because he was so lovable, earnest, and good-natured, Stephen and I worked willingly together for his best interests.

We learned that Buster might seize if things were stressful. Stephen's loud rap made Buster twitchy, a sign we learned might bring on a seizure. Shouting drove him trembling into a corner.

We adjusted the music and our tempers. If Stephen and I disagreed about something, we kept our voices calm, or stepped outside to figure it out.

In our efforts to care for Buster, we needed to keep in touch with the other's schedule. The fall Buster came to live with us Stephen convinced me that beepers for both of us were a good idea.

I didn't like the idea of beepers. Unless one was a doctor, beepers seemed to suggest illicit activities. Stephen's friends at the Park School had used beepers for such purposes. And I knew that teachers at the high school frowned on them.

But in those first months when we were learning to care for Buster, Stephen convinced me. And so we purchased a pair of beepers, opened an account, invented codes for each other, and used them to communicate.

Each time Stephen's beeper was confiscated at school, I called, to the surprise of the counselors, to say that Stephen owned the beeper with my permission, that he needed it to communicate with me regarding our epileptic bulldog, and may he please have it back?

And Stephen learned not to flaunt the instrument, or allow friends to call him at school. "They could take it away for good," he said one night. "And then how would I know if Buster needed me?"

Through Ed's intervention and our love for G.Q., Rufus, Mugs and her kittens, and now Buster, we began to create a home, a family of humans and other beings caring for each other. There turned out to be no one Stephen trusted more with Buster than me, and vice versa. I might not always trust Stephen with my car, trust his efforts in school, that he would, as he'd promised, clean out the gutters, shovel the driveway, or rake the leaves.

But I knew I could trust him to see to Buster's best interests, trust he would give him the right medications, limit Buster's playtime with the ball, and know exactly what to do if and when he seized.

Pulling in our driveway from New Hampshire with Buster, I'm greeted by Stephen and a boy who introduces himself as Trevor. They help me unload the car, pet and play with Buster. Then Stephen takes me aside.

"Mom," he says. "Now, Mom, listen. I've got to talk to you about something important."

"Okay." I take a deep breath. I'm beginning to know this preamble well.

"Promise you won't interrupt."

"Okay."

"Say you promise."

"I promise."

"Okay. Mom, Trevor's homeless."

"What?"

"You promised."

"Sorry."

"You're forgiven. Mom, listen. He's homeless. He can't go home. He's been kicked out. He's been away this whole past year at DYS. I knew him a little last summer, but then he got shipped off."

"May I ask for what?"

"You can ask. Things."

"What things?"

"Things, Mom. Stuff like I've done. What does it matter? He paid his dues. He just got home from a year in juvie, but no one wants him. They say he'll just make trouble again. He's been sleeping in a friend's car. I told him *maybe* he could stay here—just for a night or two. Mom, I'll cook the dinner. I'll make it fair, Mom."

"Just for a night or two," I answer. "We've got a lot going on, huh? School's just started. I'll be at Tufts three days a week now, and you've got school, and your community service, and the animals . . ."

"I know." Stephen is clear, earnest. "I've been thinking about all that. But look, Mom. We just rescued a dog who's epileptic. Here's a kid, Mom, a *kid* who's homeless . . ."

Trevor in trees / Photo by Stephen Digges

In late October Mugsie the cat gives birth to a second litter of kittens. A week later she is killed by a car on Blue
Hills Road. Trevor finds her as he walks home from God
knows where. He places her on the front step. The dogs
solemnly circle and sniff her.

It's about three in the morning of a weeknight, but
we're all up, our lights burning on through the November
night, each of the boys carrying out some business of his
own, music or reading. I've been what might roughly be
called asleep, released for a while upstairs like a flag at
the top of the house.

Stephen kneels and weeps. He lifts Mugs's head to see
and to show her slack gaze, the small stretched body pool-
ing a bit. Steve gently turns her over.

Trevor curses and goes to his room. Later we will hear
from him bitterly. We're still getting to know each other,
though he's lived with us now for a year.

Things hadn't gone well regarding his return home to his family from DYS. After a month or so it was clear that if he didn't stay on with us, he'd be returned to the Department of Youth Services shelter in Springfield. Though he was living at our house, attending high school with Stephen, I had no authority to speak with his teachers about his work, his status.

"I'm sorry," the guidance counselor would say, flatly satisfied, "but you have no rights in this matter."

In the end I applied to the state boards to become his foster mother.

At sixteen, Trevor is quiet, thoughtful by nature, an observer of life. It's hard for me to imagine him acting out the trouble everyone, including the school, holds against him. He loves the animals, especially the cats, and he has given African names to several.

One must look closely into his dark eyes to get a fix on his mood. He is polite, solitary, powerful in his silences.

I've begun to think of him as our Queequeg. Who can explain it? His presence has completed the circle around us. Trevor and Stephen call each other brothers, defend the other in all things. By way of their pact, they are willing to take on new responsibilities.

They work together for hours making music, beats, sampling, and Trevor is brilliant in his rap freestyling. Words come out of his mouth in a deep baritone that resonates a sadness and a will, an intimation of the islands his absent father immigrated from. Listening to Trevor freestyle, I've come to believe in the phenomenon of the gift of speaking in tongues.

Now from his room comes a loud thud. Maybe he's hit the wall with his fist.

Charles lays his hand on Stephen's head and looks hard at me. We read the other's thoughts.

"I guess we could try an eyedropper with milk," I say. "But can kittens drink cow's milk?"

"We could mix it with water and a little sugar," Charles answers.

"And warm it up," I say. "We'll get a book tomorrow. We'll ask the vet . . ."

"Can I stay home from school?" Stephen holds the dead cat in his arms. I look at poor Mugs and the blond head of the boy kneeling over her, that head with such an inventive haircut—shaved bald on the sides with a sort of mane ridging the top. Trevor hits the wall again. The buzz of the halogen light behind us burns on conspicuously, expensively, as it does every night near 3:00 A.M.

I'm aware of a sort of dream-portent, a forerunning into the crazy imminent dawn-to-day, a day through which large adolescent boys sleep on, their backpacks full of unopened schoolbooks by the door. Six tiny kittens cry to be fed while our dogs romp, slide through the kitchen, our other cats leap through the kitchen window, then out again, knocking Buster the bulldog's many epilepsy medication bottles into a sinkful of dirty dishes.

"You've missed a lot of school already," I sigh. He and I know I'm stating the obvious.

"So? For God's sake, Mom." Stephen's tears come freely. Everything about his demeanor insists that *this* above all incidents, accidents, illnesses, or just plain fatigue is the exception to beat all exceptions. This is *it* and I as his mother am missing the point.

"Look," Charles offers, "I'll run by school and pick up their work."

"Uh-huh." Something sharpens in me. "Who in the world let Mugs out? How did she get out? She was supposed to stay in the basement. We were supposed to keep that door shut."

"We need to figure out about feeding the kittens," says Charles. "Who knows how she got out? No one did it intentionally. Steve, go get a box and some blankets."

Charles has been home now for a week or so. For the past year and a half he has been living and working for a human rights organization in St. Petersburg, Russia. Now he is on leave until January. I'm thrilled to have him home and at the same time I find myself oddly self-conscious around my reasonable, conscientious, worldly, grown-up son. Life is so crazy around here. I wonder if he can adjust.

At twenty-four Charles is tall and handsome, unshaven and swarthy these days as he gets over the huge time change from St. Petersburg to Amherst. He has always been disciplined, enthusiastic, capable. I'm afraid he actually believes that with his influence now the sixteen-year-old Trevor and seventeen-year-old Stephen will turn a corner.

The most trouble—that I'm aware of—Charles has ever been in took place some years ago while he was studying in London. He and some friends climbed over the wall into the Regent's Park Petting Zoo. More than a little intoxicated, Charles fell asleep among the young goats and sheep. He was awakened by a guard who took him to jail for the night. The next morning he was released with a warning, the incident merely *noted*.

Charles is at heart philosophical, a peacemaker. He wrestles with his nature.

"Never mind," I say. "Steve, go to bed. Maybe you can go to school at noon."

"What about Trev?"

"He can go at noon, too."

"What will you tell school?" Stephen wipes his nose on his sleeve.

"I'll tell them the truth for once," I say.

"Don't," says Stephen.

"You're right," I say. We don't explain why to each other. There's no need. The boys have been absent or late to school so often, I've surely run out of believable excuses. But to tell the truth about Mugsie and be laughed at seems disrespectful of the dead cat. In our collective sense of the present scheme of things it appears, in this case, more moral to lie.

Recently I've written, *Please excuse Stephen and Trevor for being tardy. Our dogs got loose and the boys helped me to round them up...*

Another note read, *Please excuse Stephen and Trevor for being absent. Our electricity went out during the night and so our alarms didn't go off.*

And still another quite recent one said, *Please excuse Stephen and Trevor for being tardy. Our cat Mugs gave birth to six kittens last night and we stayed with her until the early hours of the morning to make sure she was ok...*

Most of the excuses I write for the boys approach truth; some are absolutely correct. Others, out of necessity, do juggle time, context. We know we've gone off the maps, off the maps and beyond the margins into that region where once the ancient cartographers wrote, *Out here there be dragons.*

The boys and I are still for a few minutes. Trevor's room has gone silent. Stephen hands the dead Mugs over to me, all the while petting her head. I hold her close. She is still warm, limp against my chest.

Our huge yard is knee-deep in leaves from our sycamores, maples, beeches. Lord knows when we'll get them raked. The gardens have dried up for the year. That sea of leaves rustles at the far dark corners where Mugsie's older offspring hunt mice or voles. We will wake to those prizes in the morning, our cats carrying their kills into the kitchen or right up the stairs and onto our pillows. November is a fruitful month for the hunters. Maybe that is what drew Mugs out. Tomorrow I'll collect the kills and set them on Mugs's grave.

Life is so big at our house, I'd like to write the attendance office. *Sometimes it is very big. Do you understand.*

We line the bottom of a dresser drawer with Stephen's old baby blankets, blankets that have somehow made the move with us from California to Missouri to Iowa to England to Maryland to Brookline and then Amherst. Several are hand-crocheted, gifts of fellow air force wives so many years ago.

The six tiny kittens curl up in one corner, a black-and-white swirl, their markings an amazing variation, as if one kitten had borrowed from the last some incidental trait, the incidental becoming all in the next, and so on.

Bette Davis, the only female, is black except for a tiny white spot on her right cheek, giving her the appearance of a chorus girl. Mugsie II has the identical markings of his mother. He is black except for white feet, and a white mask across his face.

The biggest at birth, whom Stephen names Einstein, is essentially white with black spots. He has a large black patch over one eye like a pirate. Then there is Ignaz, a gray-black tiger, and Badger, white with Ignaz's tiger stripes drawn beautifully, like a badger's mask, across his face.

The kitten Vasco DaGama is identical to the cat who impregnated Mugsie. We have seen the father in the woods behind our house, and later I see his picture at the vet's on an adopt-a-pet poster.

The vet has given the stray father a name, Rainier, as if he understands that this cat is surely the prince of Amherst, no doubt the father of much of the feral and domestic cat population in the area. He has an unforgettable face—his head is hooded in black, like an old flying ace. The rest of his face is white except for a black oval on his nose, and arched black brows.

So named by Charles, Vasco is always climbing up over his brothers and sister, out of the drawer onto the floor. There he lifts his little quivering blind head and, mewing furiously, struggles forward. When we get up through the night to feed the kittens, we often find Vasco a good distance from the drawer. We have gated the dining room against the dogs, but we worry that Vasco might stray near the mesh and wood partition and be swooped up by Rufus the basset hound.

After all, Rufus *is* a hound, by nature a hunter and a killer of small animals. From time to time he has picked up the scent of a rabbit and taken off baying, howling through the woods.

Rufus has caught and killed rabbits, moles, mice. I've seen him stalk and catch a chipmunk, shake it, and then—as if in disdain for such an easy catch—toss its broken body into the air.

We quote from a movie, *The Long Riders*, in which the outlaw Cole Younger says to Belle Starr, "You're a whore, Belle. You'll always be a whore. That's what I love about you." We change the quote slightly for Rufus:

"You're a hound, Ru. You'll always be a hound. That's what we love about you."

The bulldogs Buster and G.Q. are no threat to the kittens. Sometimes we let them through the gate to say hello and to acclimate to the new arrivals. The bulldogs sniff the kittens with passing interest and then they are content to be led out of the room.

We've tried putting Rufus on a tight leash, but once in the room with the kittens, he pulls hard toward the drawer, his face lean and otherworldly. He looks to be on the hunt, and in a rush we drag him, protesting, back across the bare wood floor and outside the gate where he pines and howls—long and lamenting—as only a basset hound can.

When I arrive home from the university in the evenings, Charles, Stephen, and Trevor greet me like new fathers, dish towels over their shoulders. They hold close a kitten who feeds on one of the baby bottles the vet has given us. I prepare a bottle, lift another of the kittens from the drawer, and join them.

We sway together in the dining room, talking over the day, feeding kittens, consorting, worrying over one or the other who seems to us just now a bit listless. We plan dinner, deciding what kind of carryout sounds good.

The November dark comes on early. It will usher in the December freeze. But our dining room is brightly lit, and warm. Our house, like a pleasure boat, throws a wide light across the leaf-strewn lawn.

From the basement we've hauled up a humidifier and two old area heaters once so necessary to us in our cold apartment in Brookline. Now they are essential to our nursery, though the heat and humidity bring out the room's new odors of milk, urine, and feces. The kittens are so tiny that on their own they can't yet pass water or defecate.

When each of us finishes feeding a kitten, we massage the little belly over a paper towel as we mimic as best we can a mother cat's tongue. The kittens move their bowels.

When Charles first demonstrated the procedure the vet had shown him, Trevor and Stephen swore off this task.

"Gross!" they chorused as, laughing, whooping, they'd backed away over the gate. Later, clearly affected by the crying as one by one the kittens waited for Charles or me to feed and massage them, the boys overcame their squeamishness.

With their help the task of feeding the kittens goes quickly. Cleaning them up, however, takes a while. With disposable wipes, then a dry towel, we rub the kittens down.

So far all are healthy, eating well, and growing rapidly, but they are a sight, a mound of fat-bellied wild-haired ragamuffins who, yawning, climbing over one another, mew loudly in the blankets as they settle in to sleep.

Now the boys head upstairs to take turns in the shower. I grab my car keys and head out the door to pick up the pizza and salad.

We're in a bit of a hurry one particular evening. As we stand eating our dinner over paper towels, Eduardo Bustamante arrives, as expected, with five or six boys

in tow. Mouths full, we greet each other; Stephen
and Trevor lead the crew into the basement where
tonight they will broadcast a radio show from Stephen's
room.

The radio show is a recent phenomenon. Having se-
cured an AM frequency on a local channel, Eduardo di-
rects a freewheeling couple of hours once a week during
which the boys play music and respond to questions and
ideas he raises regarding school, race, girls. Or the boys
themselves have topics to air.

I'm listening tonight, but at the top of the basement
steps, the kitten Bette Davis held against my chest. Earlier I noticed how much smaller, suddenly, she is than
her brothers.

I've called the vet, and though it's after eight already,
he has agreed to meet me at his office in a few minutes
to look her over, give her fluids and a shot to increase
her appetite.

The boys and Eduardo sit along the wall. They hand
the mike off to one another and nod their heads to music.
Most if not all the boys participating in the show consider
themselves outsiders to the Amherst community. Many
have been in trouble with the law. Some have dropped out
of high school. One of the purposes of the broadcast is to
give the boys a platform from which to air grievances and
search for answers.

The boys are certainly treated unfairly, baited, and singled out because of their school and community records,
and because some are African Americans. Recently the
boys were stopped by police for "a bent license plate" on
their way to attend the community college in Greenfield.

The police detained them long enough that all missed their classes.

Another event involved a boy who stepped between the police and his eight-year-old brother, whom they were in the process of "searching." The police were rough with the child. They claimed he had stolen something, though their search turned up nothing. The older brother protested the search. In the end he was cuffed and charged with assault.

Once in the system, the boys are dealt with severely. A white boy—Stephen, for instance—might be given probation and community service hours for some offense, but the African-American boys are too often given mandatory time in a grim Massachusetts detention center.

Such was the case with Trevor, once sentenced to a year in DYS. During that time, not only did he live among the toughest and most hardened of inmates, he fell far behind in school.

When he returned to the community he was marked as trouble. Written off by the public school officials, Trevor was to be enrolled in Amherst's "annex school," a sort of way station for kids to sit out the years before their sixteenth birthdays, at which time it's legal for them to quit school altogether.

We fought successfully for his right to remain in the high school. But he'd missed and lost skills, particularly in math and science. The stigma that surrounded Trevor complicated and thwarted his academic efforts.

As part of the radio broadcast, the boys recall for their listeners their trip to Washington where they participated in the Million Man March. They had planned to take one of the free buses chartered from Amherst to Washington, but the buses grew overcrowded. The organizers decided that certain people would have to be put off. To begin, anyone under eighteen had to step down.

The boys returned to our house. How they'd looked forward to this, planned, taken time off from their jobs. How badly they'd wanted to be a part of this historic event in which African-American men from all over the country came together.

I'd offered that maybe there was another way to get there. So we had checked on train schedules, other public buses departing the area, but as the boys pooled their resources, they discovered they didn't have enough money among them for each to buy a ticket.

What about if they rented a car? Emecca and Yusef had licenses. We called the local rent-a-car but we were told that the driver must be twenty-one and that he needed a credit card.

Well, then, did they know anyone who might lend them a car, I'd asked. And so six big boys climbed into my Honda Civic that Thursday evening and drove to Washington.

Their descriptions of the Million Man March dovetails into a discussion about the boys' local heroes. One is a lawyer in town named Tom Whitney. Many times he has acted on their behalf. They offer his name to their listeners in the event someone needs defending in a court of law.

Tom knows Stephen and me. We met a few years ago when Steve began his forty-five hours of mandatory community service. Steve was assigned to work at the

Amherst College planetarium. There, every Friday night, attorney at law and amateur astronomer Tom Whitney put on shows for the public.

Steve and other boys on probation helped Tom set up the planetarium shows, select the program, and run the projector. For this they received credit toward their community service hours.

Of an evening the subject of Tom's show might be comets and meteors, another night how the constellations are mapped and the meaning of their names.

One night Tom assigned Stephen the constellation of Orion, and when the lights went out and the stars appeared on the ceiling, it was Stephen who explained to the handful of viewers the story of the warrior and his dog.

Tom Whitney has helped most if not all the boys in the basement at one time or another, charging—if they can pay at all—a minimal fee, chastising them vigorously for their offenses, and defending them, he's fond of saying, as sincerely as they are sorry for whatever it is that they have done.

One by one the boys give testimonials regarding Tom as I tuck the kitten Bette Davis in a blanket under my coat and head for the vet's.

When I return all the kittens are stirring, revving up for the ten o'clock feeding. Charles isn't back yet from visiting friends, and the radio show drones on in the basement. I'm walking on top of a reggae beat. Outside the gate Rufus begins his low moaning.

"What is it you *want?*" I ask Rufus as I set Bette Davis in among her siblings and anticipate the marathon feed alone. Rufus sits up now, glad at last to be addressed. He's lain sentinel all evening.

"All right," I say, picking up the choke leash and slipping it around Rufus's neck. "Let's see what you're going to do." As usual, once in the gate Rufus tugs toward the kittens.

But this time, instead of pulling him back in a panic I control his progression as he strains to put his head in the drawer. Rufus sniffs the kittens, apparently without guile, and moves them around a bit with his muzzle.

"Careful," I warn. But to my surprise, he begins licking them gently, one then another, turning them over carefully as he licks them clean, top to bottom.

My grasp tight around the leash, I lean away from Rufus, pick up a bottle, and begin to feed Bette Davis, whose appetite is surely increased, then I set her down.

Rufus leans to the sickling. He performs deftly a mother cat's task. As the kitten's bowels relax, Rufus cleans her up, waits a moment, then licks her down again as he nudges her over to a warm corner of the drawer and awaits the next one.

And so, one by one, Rufus and I tend to the kittens. Still blind, they mew and lean toward his heat, work their way against his tongue, his hound's long nose and strong odors as he cleans and nuzzles and slides them over.

To the last bars of Marley's "War," the radio show breaks up and the boys clomp up the stairs. They linger in amazement on the other side of the gate as they watch Rufus climb into the drawer and settle carefully among the kittens.

"Word," they address Rufus. "Good man. Way to go, brother," they gently praise him.

Tired from his long watch, tired from desire and longing against our human assumptions, Rufus looks up at the boys and sighs. Then he rests his head on the edge of the drawer above his brood and falls asleep.

* * *

Dear Mr. P———,

*Having been away until two days ago, I had not received
the waiver denial regarding my son Steve Digges in Ms.
S———'s Anthropology class. This denial of waiver dis-
tresses me greatly. We can certainly document the reason
for the eleven absences in Ms. S———'s class, and intend
to do so straight away so that he may receive credit.*

*There is no doubt that one of the absences recorded in
Ms. S———'s class was the result of an in-house suspension which Stephen received for very poor judgment regarding riding on the hood of someone's car in the high school
parking lot.*

*Though Steve asked Ms. S——— to confirm dates with
him, she refused. According to the ARHS handbook, in-
house suspension absences do not count.*

Steve's Special Ed teacher attempted to intervene

and advocate for Steve with Ms. S———. Neverthe-
less, she insisted on yet another letter regarding his
absences.

Thus, at the end of the school year, we wrote a second
letter regarding a waiver for her class, and at this time
referred her to Steve's therapist's official letter that had
been submitted some time earlier (see enclosed
documents)....

Dear Amy,

Thank you for looking after things while I'm away!
Now unfortunately, if these medications aren't regularly
and consistently given, Buster will have an epileptic
seizure and go in and out of fits for about twenty-four
hours. So PLEASE make sure he gets all of his medications!

BUSTER'S MEDICATIONS

Before 8 A.M.: first thing when Buster gets up he needs 2
phenobarbital (white pills). You can hide them in a Pupperoni or a hot dog. Then he needs to eat. Then walk. Best thing
to do is to get up and do this, then go back to bed if you want!

Sometime midmorning, between 10 and 11: Buster gets a
diazepam (1 blue-green pill).

At about 5:30 or 6 P.M. just before his dinner, he gets another 2 phenobarbital. In his dinner he gets 1.6 mg of potassium bromide.

About 9:30 (before sleep) he gets 1 more phenobarbital.

ABOUT ALL DOGS:

All dogs receive a can of wet food 2 times a day. Each also gets a good handful of dry food with the wet. They eat about 7:30 A.M. and again at about 5:30 or 6:00 P.M.

Please keep plenty of fresh water available since Buster drinks large amounts of water. Also, don't forget to offer him Gatorade at mealtime.

Dogs should be walked about three times a day. One of those walks should be a good romp with a ball or a stick. Last walk can be about 8:30 or 9:00. Buster likes to sleep on my bed but needs help up.

Buster is fine off the leash, but G.Q. runs at cars and Rufus will wander off. They can be off the leash in the backyard, but watch them. They're devils!

In the event that Buster should for some reason go into seizure, just love and pet him through it, then when he comes to, give him a diazepam (extra, yes) and call Dr. Katz.

CATS

The cats like to come in and out the kitchen window. They always have dry food and 2 times a day split a can of wet food.

My number at the conference is ————. Feel free to call anytime if you have a question or a problem. . . .

Dear Registry,

This letter confirms that I have lost my license. Since my license has been suspended for sixty days, I turn in this document in its place. Thank you for your attention and patience.

Sincerely,
Stephen P. Digges

Dear Franchise Tax Board:

Enclosed is the Head of Household Audit, which you requested regarding taxes on a poetry prize awarded me by the Claremont Colleges there in California. Also as requested, I have enclosed a copy of my divorce decree and the transfer of property given to me as Grantee. Enclosed also is the first page of my taxes for 1996 with the name of my tax person at H & R Block, the person who has prepared my taxes for the last three years, each year listing me correctly as head of household.

The only people who have lived with me in the last three years are my son Stephen Digges and, from 1994 to 96, my foster son, Trevor Clunes. I did not claim Trevor as a dependent during these years because the state did pay child support for some of the time he was with us.

Sincerely...

To: Trevor and Stephen:

DAILY STUFF:

1. Feed all animals and medicate dogs. (It is SO important that Buster get his meds between 7 and 8 in the morning! Hard as it is to get up, just do it, and then go back to bed!)

2. Water gardens (in front of house, in corner of yard, AND geraniums out back).

3. Walk dogs for a good 40 minutes, either by taking them to the stables, OR walking them down the street and back (Rufus MUST be on a leash on street).

EVERY TWO- TO THREE-DAY STUFF:

1. Change cat litter boxes.

2. Water plants in new room (take out back and water with watering can or hose).

3. Check upstairs dehumidifiers and empty.

4. Put sprinklers on for front lawn grass and new grass over in corner.

LITTLE REMINDERS, HELPFUL HINTS:

The more often you change the litter boxes, the easier it is to clean them up.

Take in mail, keep it all together.

Try to keep little things—cat balls, bottle caps, etc.—off floor since Buster might eat them.

Keep counters in kitchen free of dirty dishes and sticky stuff to keep away ants.

Hang out upstairs at night as much as possible and give Buster, especially, lots of affection. Feel free to change my sheets and sleep upstairs in my room!

Maria will be here on Tues. or Wed. so try to straighten up for her....

DEBORAH DIGGES

Dear Mr. P————:

I am writing regarding my son Stephen Digges. We are requesting that you allow him a waiver of his absences, which have exceeded the allotted twenty for the year. The courses in which he has exceeded twenty absences are listed on the waiver sheet.

Stephen has had a difficult but exciting and rewarding year. To begin, I was unaware, until his Accounting teacher Mr. H———— mentioned the possibility to me in conference this past fall, that Stephen, as a student with attention deficit disorder, could be part of ARHS's IEP. I had consulted with Ms. M———— last spring about Stephen's clinical and psychological evaluations through his therapist, but I was not told at that time that in the public schools such a program existed.

I would add that since January I have also employed a tutor who works with Stephen four hours a week.

I hope that you will carefully consider Stephen's progress, his maturity, and his recent upswing toward achievement. It would be a terrible shame for him to lose credit because of his absences. He is a spirited and gifted child who has taken a little longer than most to find his way....

Dear Mr. C———,

Thanks so much for your recent letter. Enclosed are
Trevor's transcripts for this year to date, his basic skills
tests, and a photo.

Your concern about his academic status is on the mark!
And after talking again with his guidance counselor this
morning, this is the situation. If Trevor successfully com-
pletes his credits at Wolfeboro he will be close to moving
on to junior status. But he will still be lacking in credits
if and when he has completed his work at Wolfeboro. Perhaps another summer school (at Wolfeboro again next
summer?) will bring him up to his appropriate class
standing.

I wanted you to know that I have spoken with the Ed-
ucational and Instructional Director at ARHS to BE
SURE that all credits from Wolfeboro will transfer back,
and there is absolutely no problem on this. It might help,
however, were you to call Mr. P——— as you offered,
to confirm. Many times this year we have felt as if we
were pushing against a system that, no doubt unintention-
ally, overlooked Trevor's needs. No IEP was in place for
him, etc., and it took us nearly the whole year to see that
through.

Though Trev has done poorly in school, a healing has
and continues to take place in him, and as I tell him, this
year he got an A in life! He has been feeling much better
about himself, has always been wholly cooperative within
the household, and now I begin to see a joy in living come
through his eyes! He is VERY excited and committed to the
Wolfeboro Program.

We look forward to hearing from you regarding a schedule, and many, many thanks for all you have done and continue to do.

Sincerely…

P.S. Trev is scheduled for his physical on Mon., May 15, so as soon as we have all the documentation I'll send this on. I am also hoping that the state will help to fund some of Trevor's tuition and have been working hard at this end to see this through, so if monies come in in fits and starts, please be patient! We will have it paid in full as soon as possible!

Dear Attorney Whitney,

I want to thank you once again for coming to Steve's aid. I would add that with this exception, he has done so very well in getting his life straightened out. He has worked hard in school and made the honor roll this semester!

Recall that his probation was completed a year and a half ago and since then there has been no trouble with the law until now. During his probation, as you remember, he did community service at the planetarium. I have copies of his work papers on file.

I should tell you too that Steve successfully completed driver's retraining education last spring at Holyoke Community College.

Secondly, though he had not paid the fees to reinstate his license, he had not driven during his 60-day suspension. This incident followed that 60-day period.

Also, the policeman who arrested him said that Steve was exceptionally polite and cooperative upon arrest.

I'm afraid I have the flu and am pretty sick or I would be there with you.

Sincerely ...

DEBORAH DIGGES

To: Franchise Tax Board:

*Before I pay the amount supposedly due on this document,
I am to be informed of the results of the Head of Household Tax audit which your people are performing at present. When the results of this particular issue are laid to
rest, it may be that you will need to refund the $500.00 I
sent you.*

*Please pay attention to former correspondence, docu-
ments and information regarding my account....*

*How to set coffee timer so that you will have coffee when
you wake up:*

1. Set timer to Off.

2. Set coffee machine to On.

3. Fill coffee machine with water.

4. Put filter in and coffee.

*BE SURE TIMER IS SET TO OFF,
AND COFFEE MACHINE TO ON!
Wake up and smell the coffee!*

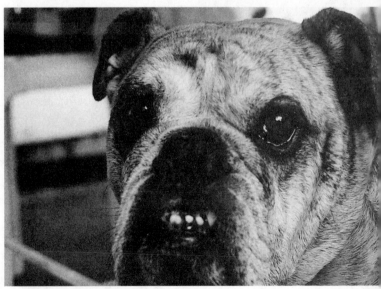

Portraits of Rufus and Buster / Photos by Stephen Digges

The last gift I happen to give Stan before he leaves is a plum tree that he planted in our yard in Amherst. It's a stunted little sapling that barely survives its first winter. But in the early summer, our divorce pending, there it is, putting out a few white blossoms.

I decide to pull the thing out of the ground. I want no reminders of our life together, a life too full of departures. The sad little tree with its sparse sprigs is testament to the emptiness both of us lived with through the eight years of our long-distance marriage.

Wearing big gloves, shovel in hand, I head for the tree one afternoon. I'm going to dig it up, blossoms and all, and toss it far back into the woods. At first I try simply pulling it out of the ground, grabbing the trunk with both hands, stripping as I do the few blossoms from the shoots. But it won't give.

I try again, this time heaving and shaking the trunk to

loosen the roots. Then I pick up the shovel and begin banging it against the trunk, grab it again, and heave.

It's one of the first summer days, late June, most of the foliage out, the air alive with seed fluff and down, a day in which you sense the certainty of the green world. Memory for the stingy cold of the previous winter has almost disappeared, and there's an arrogance in you. You can be careless with the green.

I grab the trunk of the tree close to the ground and pull with all my strength, pull to feel the effort wholly, my weight pitted against it. I exert to the point of bloodrush blindness and deafness, groan and heave. I don't hear Stephen shouting until he's next to me.

"Mom! Stop! Mom! What are you doing!"

Stephen grabs my shoulders and I turn surprised and out of breath. It's Saturday. As usual, he slept late, and he appears now in boxer shorts, his hair sticking out at angles, his young face always younger upon waking.

"I'm getting rid of it," I huff. "I don't want it in our yard."

"It's just a tree!" he says, and as he speaks I witness my son's avocation, deep surprise at his mother who would pull a tree out of the ground in an attempt to even some score. He is ashamed of me, his beautiful blue eyes full of hurt; he seems to search past me to find some other woman inside my eyes, someone he can recognize and appeal to.

I let go of the tree and step away. Despite my efforts, it stands rooted, however stripped.

"Anyway," I offer as I wipe my sweaty hair back from my face, "it won't give."

As if to prove it for himself, Stephen reaches to it and gives the trunk a light tug.

"Ya," he says. "I think it's okay."

We stand silent a few moments looking at the tree, then at each other. Stephen breaks into a wide grin and begins to laugh.

"Mom," he says. "What in the hell were you doing?"

"I was trying to get rid of this tree."

"I know, but *what* were you doing?"

I'm silent. I don't know how to answer.

"Mom," Stephen laughs as he puts his arms around me. "Never mind. It's just a tree."

I hide my face, trying not to let Stephen see my tears.

"Aw, Mom," Stephen comforts me. He laughs again as he hugs me, then picks me up and whirls me around.

"Come on back in, Mom," he says as he sets me down. "It's okay to be sad, but we can't go pulling out trees, now can we? What would Ed say?"

"He'd say you're supposed to join me." Now I'm laughing through my tears. Stephen picks up the shovel and steps back to let me go first. I hesitate.

"Go on," he instructs. "Into the house, *Mother*. I'll make some coffee," he says, "and put a few armed guards on that tree."

Northampton's emergency room is crowded this Friday
night. I've been waiting over an hour to see a doctor, a
blood-soaked towel wrapped around my right wrist. I've
left a message at home for the boys explaining my departure by ambulance, along with instructions not to approach G.Q., who earlier attacked me.

The boys weren't at home at the time of the attack.
Now and then I dial the pay phone to see if anyone answers.

I hold the towel tight against my wound to keep the
bleeding down. Impatient, considering leaving the emergency room to go home and tend to the wound myself, I
open the towel to see that no, I'd better stay. The wound
is bad, the flesh torn to the bone.

I'm confused about what has happened. Against reason
my feelings are deeply hurt over the fact that G.Q. lashed
out at me. It's true that we've begun to notice changes in

him. At first we attributed those changes to the additions of Rufus and Buster to the household, not to mention the new litter of cats, whom we kept, every one. No doubt G.'s territory was impinged upon.

And yet G.'s strange behaviors seemed to have little to do with the other animals. For one thing we can no longer walk him off leash because he runs at cars. Recently he bolted straight at a neighbor passing our driveway, hit the passenger side, and bounced off. I was sure the dog was hurt, but on the contrary, he picked himself up and walked back, undaunted, toward me.

Other times as he's sat with the kids on the floor of the living room, he suddenly stiffens. His eyes wild and remote, he begins to pant and growl and lick his lips. Recognizing danger, the boys have known to move away from him—in that split second he has lunged at one of them. Then he's walked away, as if baffled at his own behavior.

I took him to the vet, who suggested that when such an incident occurred I offer him one of Buster's Valiums.

"He might be having a kind of seizure," the vet explained. "And be careful," he warned. "This dog could be dangerous. He might just be crazy," he concluded. "These dogs are overbred. In such cases it's better to put them down."

I heard what the vet told me. At the same time I could not imagine that what he said was true, until tonight, when G. had lunged at my arm as I set his dinner bowl on the kitchen floor.

Perhaps I had unwittingly connected G.'s behaviors with Stephen's of a few years before, behaviors of aggression that have all but vanished, in part because of his love for this very dog.

G.Q. was the first being in a long time with whom Stephen authentically and positively connected. Through that connection his empathy for others was rekindled.

G.Q. taught me many things as well. The night Stan retrieved Stephen from the police station, I witnessed the dog's unconditional greeting and Stephen's response. And I had coined a phrase that night we've repeated—affecting cheer: "G. doesn't care about criminals . . ."

After the doctor cleans my wound and stitches me up, I try calling home once more, but no answer. A taxi takes me the ten miles to Amherst. Once home I mop the blood off the kitchen floor, wary of G., who greets me with the old charm and makes his way back to the living room, where he jumps up on the couch and falls asleep.

When they arrive home, Trevor and Stephen are wild with concern. Stephen makes us tea while Trevor paces, trying to make sense of what has happened.

"I don't know," I say. "I've had many dogs, Trev. But I've never seen this before."

We both look over to G.Q. Sprawled out on his back in his bed, he snores loudly.

"He can't be attacking you," Trevor states.

The next morning I call a friend of mine, the dean of the Tufts School of Veterinary Medicine in Grafton and a veterinarian himself. He and I became friends a few years ago.

We met through a review in the *New York Times* of a book I'd written. Frank read the review and noticed that I taught at Tufts on the Medford campus. Because the book, in part, described my childhood relationships with animals, the dean sent me a note through intercampus mail. In the note Frank commented on how much he liked the book, and he extended an invitation to tour the Grafton campus hospitals and wildlife clinic.

Since our meeting, Frank has come to our aid during our many animal crises. He faxed us information on how to care for our orphaned kittens, and he's kept an eye on Buster by way of sending us information regarding canine epilepsy.

Aware of the problems that Stephen encountered in Brookline, Frank also invited Stephen to visit Grafton. On one occasion we brought G.Q. with us. Frank walked us among the horses, sheep, and cow barns, sparrows sailing the wide girth of the stables.

Like me, Frank believes in the significance and healing power of human and other animal relationships. As he listens to my story of G.'s attack, I am afraid he is going to suggest, as our local vet has, that G. is too dangerous to remain with us. But Frank has another idea.

"I am going to put you in touch with our animal behaviorist here," Frank says. "Let's make the appointment right away. There still might be something we can do."

*   *   *

We live close to one another and to the animals. Stephen and Trevor share a tutor on weeknights. While they work I get dinner ready—four packages of ravioli and two boxes of broccoli dumped in boiling water that steams the kitchen windows, two loaves of bread and a salad, all of which will disappear when we sit down together in front of a fire.

Charles and I take turns feeding and walking the dogs. He usually takes them out in the mornings and midday, while I set out with them in the evenings. Often Stephen or Trevor comes with me. It's a good time to talk about problems they are having at school, or with one another.

Some of our older cats come along on our walks even when winter's at its worst. They dart far out in front to lie in wait behind a bush. As we approach they leap out to surprise us. Other times we find them lounging in the dust at the roadside.

And there is the ritual of the laundry. For most of our last two years together it must be taken to the Laundromat, our dryer hopelessly broken, in pieces on the basement floor.

Once he pronounced it unfixable, the electrician who came out to look at it left in a hurry—happy to escape what must have appeared to him a madhouse of activity and noise, the dogs joyously sniffing and circling him and his tools, the boys at work in the adjoining basement room mixing and recording, our cats batting lint balls around him as Rufus, grunting and growling, would try to corral them; Rufus, whom we believe to be going through interminable postpartum depression regarding the cats. They're fully grown and these days they mostly taunt and/or ignore Rufus, who mothered them in their orphaned infancy.

Because we don't have the money to buy a new dryer, we drop our laundry off to be done by attendants at a local Laundromat. But when we pick it up, we find notes taped to our bags that read, *Dear customer, we do not appreciate receiving dirty laundry that contains so much animal hair. Some of our staff is allergic.*

Another time a note says, *"Dear customer, the sheets in the laundry you dropped off smelled of urine. We ask that you rinse these items before giving them to us."*

"This is humiliating. Buster can't help it. They're treating us like the Snopeses," Charles says, referring to a family in Faulkner, as he unloads the bags from the car.

"I agree. We'll do it ourselves from now on," I offer.

Going to the Laundromat for a couple of hours each week actually becomes a job I look forward to. Pretty soon

Stephen comes along as we discover a shared domestic pleasure, doing such mounds and mounds of dirty laundry—six to ten loads—taking up many washers including the huge industrial ones for the sheets and blankets soiled as a result of Buster's most recent seizures; and then our plotting for an entire row of dryers, one of us standing guard while the other deftly pulls laundry out of the machines, loads up several baskets, and triumphantly rolls them over, one in each hand.

Then there's the folding, which we enjoy most, folding clean, fresh-smelling sheets and towels, shirts, pants. The trunk I once packed full of clothes for Stephen has long since been ransacked for Trevor. As luck would have it, Trevor and Stephen are about the same size. The trunk serves as Trev's dresser.

One night Stephen and I find ourselves folding a run of twenty or so identical boxer shorts complete with sports insignia.

"Where did these come from?" I ask.

"I think they're a *gift* from Trevor," he answers. "I guess you won't have to buy us underwear for a long time. I saw another couple of boxes of these in the garage . . ."

Besides maintenance and upkeep of the house, work, and schoolwork, our animals teach us rituals. Rufus loves to howl. He possesses a hound's deep baritone and will "sing" on command, sing passionately, starting in the lower octaves and reaching crescendos that so amaze and move us, we reward him with almost a whole pack of Pupperoni, the other dogs rewarded in the wake of Rufus's performance simply for being Rufus's friends.

And Buster, indeed, loves balls. At the sight of one he

cannot be distracted. He is compulsive about balls, perhaps owing to his epilepsy. Buster must be kept indoors if
the boys decide to shoot baskets in front of the garage or
he will steal the ball and boot it all the way down the hill
to the retirement home.

Now and then we let him have the ball inside our
fenced yard, but he's allowed to play with it for fifteen,
at the most twenty minutes at a time or he will pop it,
and/or bloody his nose, and/or work himself into such
a frenzy he begins to seize.

As for G.Q., the behaviorist at the vet school in Grafton
diagnosed him as dominant aggressive, a condition, he
told us, that often surfaces about the time a dog reaches
two years old.

"If he were in the wild, he would be alpha male, top
dog," he explained.

"In the wild," I considered. "He's not far from it . . ."

To suppress his aggression, the behaviorist instructed
us, we must engage G. in rigorous training, including disciplined walks on the leash followed by the exercise of
the command of fifty to one hundred downs each day.
The behaviorist also put him on Prozac.

All of us participate in G.'s training lest he get the no-
tion he can bully any of us. During the early dark, sleet or
snowfall, while I cook dinner or while the tutor instructs
one or the other, the boys work with the bulldog in the
dining room. Rufus and Buster drop in and try a few
downs themselves. Over the drone of the tutor's explana-
tions of algebraic equations can be heard: "G., heal! Good
boy! G.Q., down! Good boy! Buster, down. Good boy! Rufus, down. Rufus, down. Rufus, *down* . . ."

My friend Frank has sent us a video showing the beneficial effects of Prozac on animals. One weekend my sister Eve comes to visit, and while she and I shuck a huge barrel of corn, I show her the video. We listen to the narrator explain how a bird, once confined in a cage much too small for him, plucked out all of his feathers. Though the bird was rescued and moved to a larger cage, he continued to torment himself and was nearly bald, full of scabs and scrapes.

Given careful doses of Prozac, however, the bird is shown in various stages as he grows new feathers, until at last he is fully arrayed, content, and animated. You can see for the first time that the bird is a beautiful parrot.

"I've known people like that," says Eve, a practicing psychologist now in divinity school.

Another segment of the video shows a dog who refuses to come out from behind the drapes of his person's living room, and yet another dog who has fixated on a particular stick and cannot be persuaded to put it down. As a result that dog hardly eats or sleeps.

"That's me," I comment.

"I'm the one behind the curtain," Eve answers.

Once on Prozac, however, both dogs behave more normally—the first now happy, apparently, to be a part of the household as he naps in the center of the living room. The second dog is clearly uninterested in the stick to which earlier he was enslaved.

The voice on the video discusses each case, comparing the bird with others confined too closely who did not pluck out their feathers.

And why, the commentator asks, did the first dog feel that he was only safe behind the drapes? Why did the second dog fixate on the stick while another happily gave it up to his person, played with other sticks, then abandoned them to go inside?

It is hard to say, the voice explains. Perhaps these animals lack the necessary serotonin, were born with low levels. Close captivity appears to have depleted the once-healthy bird's levels. After rescue, he still could not recover without help from the drug.

Prozac seems to be working for G.Q. Since he has been taking capsules in a piece of bologna every morning, we haven't observed him going strange, stiffening, narrowing his eyes, and licking his lips, though Stephen, if he is irritated about something, adopts the gesture.

Portrait of Frank / Photo by Stephen Digges

1. **Mettle:** *The boys jumped from rooftop to rooftop showing off their* **mettle** *to the onlookers below.*

2. **Dour:** *Her expression was* **dour** *when she told me I was going to fail the quarter.*

3. **Beguile:** *The boys would* **beguile** *the cops into believing that the fire was electrical.*

4. **Ogle:** *Her shapely figure caused her students to* **ogle** *blatantly.*

5. **Cull:** *Ms. A. has chosen to* **cull** *me out of the rest of the group as someone whose excuses are unacceptable.*

6. **Deleterious:** *The entire concept of grading the individual according to a standardized system can cause a* **deleterious** *self-esteem problem.*

7. **Doleful:** *His expression was doleful as he was led into the police station.*

8. **Ameliorate:** *He would **ameliorate** his friends' problems by stealing a car to drive them home.*

9. **Reticent:** *The **reticent** man turned out to be a spy.*

10. **Subvert:** *With the help of many I will **subvert** the present social and political systems.*

11. **Raze:** *The kid will **raze** his room in anger if he isn't let out soon.*

* * *

Arrested once more for driving on a suspended license, Stephen walks in the door one evening. He's bailed *himself* out of jail, perhaps a good thing for him to know how to do.

Shaking his head, he quotes from the movie *Jaws*: " 'Sometimes the sharks go away.' " he says. " 'Sometimes they *don't* go away.' "

Another evening Trevor storms in the door, furious with the teachers at Amherst Regional High. He spent last summer at a special camp where he not only brought up his grades, he excelled with A's in math, English, and history.

He had hoped to improve his status from eternal freshman in high school to junior or senior. When Trevor announced his plans to go to Wolfeboro School Camp in New Hampshire, the local high school suggested it might be possible, *if*, they added, he did well.

But now those teachers say no. No, his intense summer work is not enough, after all, to advance him. Even though he is much older than all of his classmates he must remain a freshman. Yes, they insist, if he wants to stay in school, he must retake his freshman year. Neither he nor I can change their minds.

Trevor's seething ignites Stephen's demonstrative anger. The two of them begin plotting to get back at the teachers. They're revving up to be sure, holding each other, conspiring.

Charles steps in and places his hands on their shoulders.

"Fellas," he begins, tuning his voice a little, mimicking the mayor in *Jaws*. Charles exaggerates his preparation to get the boys' attention. Trevor and Stephen stand back.

" 'Fellas, be reasonable. *I* for one am *not* going to *stand* here and *watch you do* some kind of *half-assed au-topsy* on a fish and see that little *Kit*-ner boy spill *out all* o-ver *this dock . . .*' "

We look to all kinds of literature, poems, and songs to find direction. Bob Marley's "You can't blame the youth, you can't fool the youth of today . . . ," and "One good thing about music . . ." are favorites. And Charles has an amazing ability to quote whole passages of prose. If I'm worried or upset about something, at my request he lovingly recites the last paragraph of Joyce's *The Dead*.

Still, *Jaws*—its plot, characters, dialogue—becomes for us a code of ethics, words to live by, much as verses from the New Testament were my mother's.

As a child I would hear my mother call out to a beautiful spring day, " 'This is the day the Lord hath made. Let us be glad and rejoice in it.' "

Our *Jaws* version is double-edged: "It's a beautiful day . . . the beaches are open . . . , " which carries the multiple meaning of "Watch your back. This could be the day of a major shark attack."

If as a child I attempted to twist the truth to turn it in my favor, my mother might have quoted, "Ye shall know the truth, and the truth shall set you free . . ."

When Stephen or Trevor offer diluted excuses, I might affect Hooper's disgust at the carnage of the first shark attack and the mayor's attempts to cover it up.

"Come off it," I say. " 'This wasn't any boating accident . . .' "

When the dishes are stacked high in the sink, the laundry piled up to mountainous proportions, when the boys are behind in their schoolwork, Buster is going through a cluster of seizures, my mother might revert to her favorite verse, Romans 8:28, a wonderful disclaimer: "For we know that all things work together for those who love God and who are called according to his purpose."

The *Jaws* version also recognizes the magnitude of the daily: "We're going to need a bigger boat."

Heading down the basement one evening to gather the boys' clothes for the laundry, I see what looks like the apocalypse escaping from beneath the storage room door, open it to find the cats basking before a great light, basking in the warmth of several huge grow-lights, the shelves inside lined with thriving illegal weed.

My mother might be reduced to the belting out the words of the prophets from the dreaded Old Testament, "Get thee down, Moses, for thy people have corrupted themselves!"

Charles, drawn downstairs by cries, shakes his head as he rubs his hands toward the warmth.

"Hmm. Well, well, well."

" 'Take a good look,' " I answer. " 'Those proportions are correct.' "

" 'Like to get your name in the *National Geographic*.' "

We stare into the brightness.

"Actually it's lovely," I say. "And *green*."

"Just listen to the electric meter ticking."

"*Busted*. They are *busted* . . ."

" 'Chief,' " Charles says, beginning to clear the shelves, " 'put out the fire, will you?' "

*　*　*

Dear Frank,

I'm so glad you'll be coming to dinner, but ever since I invited you, I've been worried sick. Maybe I haven't been entirely honest with you about the nature of this household, and thought to write to prepare you. If you decide not to come, I understand.

You should be forewarned, especially since you'll be coming on a weeknight.

This is a wild household. Dogs sleep on beds no questions asked. The boys often do their homework in my room—Steve at his word processor (his mouse Frederick in his pocket!), Trevor spread out on the floor, Buster and Rufus snoring as the pizza man arrives with dinner, cats leaping in and out of the windows (we've removed all screens for this purpose, the upshot of this that the most beautiful moths grace the walls and ceilings now and all through the summer and fall)!

There may be phone calls from teachers, more often the cops. Yes, cops. As you know Buster goes through cluster seizures, and I'm afraid he is about due.

I suppose I had some sort of fifties fantasy when I invited you out. To be honest I'm not a very involved cook, the volume of food required here forbidding little more than whole bags of things dumped in to boil.

If you'd rather not come, I understand. I'd love for you to, but I'll take it in stride if you decided against it. From what you've told me, you live a very different life.

Hey, I'm not trying to scare you, but let's not entertain false assumptions....

Sincerely,

P.S. If you decide to come, I should explain the smell in the kitchen. We've been propping the doors open each night so the dogs can go out to pee if they need to. Well, a skunk wandered in the kitchen door—probably after the cat food—and I'm afraid he sprayed. Though we've washed everything down, there's still quite an odor. At any rate, if it doesn't rain, we'll cook outside.

Dear Mr. P————,

I so enjoyed judging your poetry contest! Please let these students know that I was impressed and moved by the power of their feelings and their care with language and form. I commented on at least one poem by each poet. It was very hard to decide, and I hope it is okay with you that besides the first, second, and third place winners, I chose six honorable mentions....

PORTAL OF THE III "I" (THIRD EYE) CONTRACT

Hip-hop, reggae, and R&B are free of charge. Any deviation from this selection will result in a twenty-dollar surcharge.

1. We spend thirty minutes preview for Presentation. Beyond that time, a fifteen-dollar minimum is required.

2. A fifteen-dollar consultation fee is required.

3. All presentations are on a cash basis and require 50% deposit on all cash sales above twenty-five dollars to begin presentation jobs, such as equipment, ground space, transportation, etc. These extra costs are separate from presentation and will be paid for by client.

4. We are not responsible for any damage or other liabilities. The only responsibility pertaining to our organization is the music.

5. Our standard fee is based upon the hourly rates for work and does not include separate, pre-presentation costs.

In the event of cancellation, a fee will be charged based upon the original contract price. It is to the client's utmost

*advantage to come with information and organization to
avoid adding any time to the job structure.*

Client _____

Contractors: Stephen Digges and Trevor Clunes

Date Signed: _____

CONTRACT RATES:

HOURLY RATES: 20$
TRANSPORTATION/EQUIPMENT FEE: 30$
CANCELLATION FEE: 50% OF ORIGINAL CONTRACT FEE

Dear Trev,

While I am gone I am putting you in charge of several things:

*1. Watering and maintaining the gardens and the window
boxes. Make sure each evening all the gardens have lots of
water, and don't forget the little window boxes on the front
of the house, over by the garage, and on the back patio.*

*2. E-mailing me in Russia at least three times. I'll have
shown you exactly how to get on-line with CompuServe.
Please keep me informed of everything, send me news!*

*3. You will also be in charge of dinner on Tues., Wed., and
Sat., and Tues. night of next week (see calendar in kitchen).
Tues. and Wed., Joanne will be here, so Steve will be busy*

*with tutoring. Then he will clean up those nights and fix
dinner on other nights.*

*The nights that he fixes dinner, you are in charge of clean-
up. There will be plenty of things to eat, and it will be your
job, while Steve is with Joanne, and then later, too, to plan
and get the meal on the table for you and Steve and Brian.*

*4. Buster's hips really bother him at night so I am asking
you that while I am away, DO NOT LET HIM PLAY WITH THE
BASKETBALL! If you want to play, close the front door and
the side door, too.*

5. Keep up with your laundry and keep your room neat.

I know you can do it, and I wish you luck! I'll miss you!

Dear Mr. T————:

*I am faxing you the deed for 101 Blue Hills Road, a house
for which your company has the mortgage. Because the
house was originally in my former husband's name, it has
been difficult for me to correspond with and/or receive re-
sponses from you.*

*Yesterday I spoke with a woman at your establishment
who told me if I faxed this document to you, this information would allow me to speak about the financial status and
the mortgage status of this residence.*

*First of all, see letter and insurance document also faxed
regarding ————'s overcharging me for house insurance I
already possessed with ————. As a result, ————*

overcharged me over a thousand dollars, money that I wanted to put toward my September house payment.

I received a letter from ———— stating that they had indeed overcharged me, and that this money had been put in the escrow account. Because the house insurance was in my name and not my former husband's, I suppose my request could not be acted upon. Now I am hoping that this will change.

Secondly, while I was at work, a certified letter from ———— arrived. I suspect this is some kind of warning, though I could not pick up the letter at the post office because I am not Stanley Plumly.

Thirdly, I sent off the November payment for the house on the 7th of Nov. and ———— has not yet received it. I suggested to the woman on the phone yesterday that perhaps I should stop payment on that check and send you another. She advised me to wait a few days.

In any case, I hope that this deed/divorce settlement which deeds the house IN MY NAME will allow us to get everything straightened out regarding my mortgage status and that in the future we can speak directly about said property.

Sincerely . . .

Dear Steve,

While I am away I am putting you in charge of several things.

1. Feeding and medicating of animals AT NIGHT. This means giving Buster a diazepam at dinner, and then REMEMBERING to give him one about 9 o'clock at night.

2. VERY IMPORTANTLY YOU MUST DEPOSIT MY PAYCHECK ON WED. Carol Ann is sending it FedEx on Tues. and I am asking you to take it through the drive-thru window at the bank and get it IN the bank as soon as possible.

You can do this quickly on Wed. after school after you have checked the mail. The deposit slip is in an envelope on the kitchen table.

If you are not sure what to do, just ask the lady at the window. Tell her you want to deposit this in your mother's checking account. She will help you!

3. You will be in charge of feeding cats each evening. Split one can of cat food on two plates with a handful of dry, and also give them a big bowl of half-and-half.

4. Late in the week I am putting you in charge of doing one or two loads of towels so that you will have some! Just wash, dry, and fold, put in linen closet.

5. Be prompt for Joanne. And VERY IMPORTANT—get to school on time!

We have used up all goodwill at ARHS. Let's get through these last weeks, okay??? Good!

Stardust / Photo by Stephen Digges

Today is Stephen's eighteenth birthday. Some time ago he twisted his thick blond hair into dreds. When he grew tired of the look, he asked me to help him comb it out, but no amount of detangler or cream rinse would loosen it.

The only thing to do was to shave his head. Now, a year later, his hair is long and full. He pulls it back in a pony-tail.

Stephen loves to sun himself. Even in late autumn, wearing his Walkman, his thermal underwear, coat, and boots, he'll sit out on the patio with his homemade reflec-tor—a double album sleeve covered in tinfoil—and soak up the rays of the weak New England sun.

"He's crazy," says Trevor as we sip coffee in the kitchen.

"A little," I offer. "He was born in Southern California."

In build and gesture Stephen resembles his father. He's

about five feet ten and slim, muscular. By his eighteenth birthday he has recovered the energy and dimension that marked his childhood. He is boyish, temperamental, magnetic in his happiness and forbidding in his anger. His is a dynamic presence. He can slam a door like no other member of our household. Or he swoops in to pick me up and whirl me around the kitchen as he relays some happiness.

He is committed to our animals, whom he embraces and talks to and kisses without self-consciousness. He has an affinity and patience for the dogs and cats that do not always translate to humans. His play and affection for them is engaged and concentrated, and when he is finished, he is finished.

"Go see Mom," he says with feigned enthusiasm as he slips away and heads down to his room in the basement.

Stephen hates television, popular music, brand-name clothing, affectation. He has a keen discernment of the gestures and speech in others, and bitterly attacks them when he senses that they are behaving, as he says, "phony."

At school he does best in classes whose teachers he likes. It really doesn't matter what the subject is. And he does poorest when he suspects a teacher is condescending or coddling. In these cases he is too good at bringing them to bay, angering and exhausting them.

Stephen loves his body, loves working out alone—though not at a gym. Rather, he does pull-ups on the thick branch of the white pine out back. He has set a ladder against that tree and lashed it so that it will not give way. He climbs up high, then slips his legs through the rungs, and from a hanging position pulls himself up, his arms across his chest, his ponytail flying while below him the dogs circle, barking, and the cats perch on various rungs or on a tree limb, as if to lend him support.

He loves being clean and carries out lengthy rituals of skin and hair care, uses specified deodorants and colognes the rest of the household is not to touch. And by eighteen he has come to love to clean his room, loves to dust and vacuum and scrub. There is a sign on his door that insists that anyone entering must remove shoes. It is not a joke.

Stephen loves his camera, an old Pentax that his brother gave him. Using black-and-white film, he sets up for himself different projects, carries them out and develops the film in his darkroom. At a garage sale he found an enlarger, and the necessary pans, bins, and chemicals. He is unequivocal about not being disturbed, disappearing for hours to reappear with photos of the sky and clouds, train tracks, abandoned barns and warehouses, or various and prolific studies of weeds in winter. He says his subject is "light."

A year older than Trevor, Stephen acts as big brother, often explaining to me his analyses of Trevor's behaviors.

"Trev's a man of few words," Stephen says when I express worry over Trevor's silences. "He's not mad. He's just thinking. If you try to make him talk, he freezes. It's like when his therapist comes over. The living room," he laughs, "is completely silent! Or you hear the guy mumbling on—you hear the sound of questions—'blah, blah, blah, blah'? Silence! That's Trevor, Mom. That's his way."

That's his way ... that's her way ... Stephen has introduced this phrase to the rest of us. It means there are certain things that can't be changed about a person, and if this is so, then one must accept it, work around it, and/or ignore it. It's a phrase that preserves one's dignity, or the dignity of another, in the face of criticism.

While Stephen walked the dogs one afternoon, a school official who lives down the street confronted him.

"I need for you to know," she said, "that I have called the Department of Youth Services to say that yours is an unfit house for a foster child."

Stephen was distracted by trying to keep the dogs from peeing or pooping in her yard, a travesty she recently complained to the boys about. And he was struggling with tact, with maintaining a decorum. Not too long ago he might have told the woman to go *fuck* herself. These days he works at being what he calls a *citizen*, not necessarily because it's the right thing to do, but because, as Ed has suggested to him, "you have less to carry around."

"How do you know it's their poop?" he had asked, a question she considered insolent.

"I've studied the configurations," she answered. "I know your dogs' feces from all others . . ."

Stephen put the dogs on leashes as she continued.

"Trevor was one of my advisees before he was sent away. Long before you knew him. He needs discipline, structure. And if your mother won't tell you, I will. You two can't be out in the yard shouting and wrestling with these dogs at midnight. Nor should Trevor be shooting baskets when he's supposed to be in school."

"He doesn't like school much," Stephen offered, trying to restrain the dogs, unused to leashes in the first place.

"Doesn't *like* school?" She shook her head. "Your mother should be attending the parent-training lectures at the high school."

"Mom talks to Ed," Stephen answered.

The woman clicked her tongue.

"Tell your mother that I will be looking for her on
Monday evening. We have a guest speaker from the organization Tough Love."

"I'll give her the message." Stephen released the dogs
who tore down the street, leashes flying. "But I doubt
she'll come. It's not her way . . ."

As Stephen recounts the story to us at his birthday dinner, he is by turns furious and laughing as he reconsiders
the conversation.

"*Did* she call DYS?" Trevor asks.

"If she did, I haven't heard about it," I say. "I don't
think there's anything to worry about."

Indeed, the Department of Youth Services rarely calls
and more rarely returns my phone calls. Trevor's advocate,
a young man named Will, sounds harried and exhausted
when I speak with him. When he makes a date with
Trevor to go buy clothes or spend some time together, he
usually has to break it.

Once Trevor and I drove out to Springfield for an evaluation. We followed complicated directions to the center, a
tired series of low, sixties-style institutional outbuildings,
the dead lawns the same color as the yellow brick offices.
As we walked across the grass toward an entrance, we
were greeted by shouts from the barred windows on the
second story, boys incarcerated there, as Trevor once was,
who pressed their hands and faces to the wire.

"That's the dayroom," Trevor said as we made our way
up the sidewalk. "Also the classroom, also the cafeteria."

"Get it," I answered. "Do you know any of the guys?"

"Probably," he said. And then, "Let's get this over
with."

But as it turned out, the officials we were to see had either left for the day or couldn't be found.

"We have an appointment with Will," I'd said to a man, maybe a guard or a cop, who smoked a cigarette just outside the front door. "Here." I showed him the form with the date and the time written in.

"I don't know what to tell you," he said. "You could try that building over there." He pointed across the complex.

One by one, Trevor and I were sent to this building or that. After about an hour, we gave up. "You go ahead to the car," I said to Trev, who was tired, irritated, and embarrassed. "I'll write a note and leave it for Will."

Trevor and I were here for this appointment, I wrote on the back of the form. *We wanted you to know that we were here and ready for the evaluation. Trevor is doing well. He has just finished courses at Greenfield Community in preparation for his GED.... Please call us when you get this so that we may reschedule....*

The night of Stephen's birthday dinner—some months after our visit to Springfield—I watch Trevor's worried expression relax as we look at each other and remember our trip to DYS.

"Don't worry," I repeat and wink at Trevor.

"No, don't worry." Stephen passes the tacos. "I mean, what's she gonna say?" Stephen affects a woman's voice, pitching his own into a high whine. "Tsk, tsk, tsk. *Will.* Trevor and Stephen are having too much fun . . . I personally witnessed them rolling around in the leaves when they were supposed to be raking them . . . I personally witnessed them *breaking* their rakes . . . I heard them singing 'Happy Birthday' . . . I saw the configurations . . ."

—Stephen nearly spits food as he laughs—"of their dogs' bowel movements in my yard . . ."

"Who you gonna tell." Charles coins the phrase we've adopted in the event that someone begins to whine.

"Right!" Stephen reaches across the table to punch Trevor on the shoulder. "Who you gonna tell?" He grins, and we answer in unison, "Your guidance counselor?"

At eighteen Stephen loves the girls and the girls love him. He's had a series of girlfriends with whom, in front of all to see, he is affectionate and playful. The school has called to say that he and so-and-so are being much too amorous in the halls, engaging in kissing as one or the other goes off to class, etc. He and the girl have been called into the principal's office.

Stephen is passionate in his defenses to his teachers and to me. He is in love. Why should he behave as if he weren't?

"They're so uptight!" he explodes one night when I report that the girl's parents have called. "Man, I'm from California! Don't forget that, Mom. I was born in California. And don't forget that not so long ago right *here* they were burning witches. Yep. Just a couple of generations back, the ancestors of my teachers were burning witches. I get it. I do."

Stephen once showed a discernment about sex, however, when Mugsie gave birth to her kittens. She chose as the birth site a space under a low table covered by a sheet in Stephen's basement room. Stephen was awakened by the mewing of the first two kittens and he slipped upstairs to alert me.

"How wonderful," I'd said. "I'm coming down."

"Wait," said Stephen. "I need to prepare you. Mom, I feel terrible."

"Why?"

"Well, Mugsie is having her kittens on my stash of *Playboy*s. I hide 'em under that table . . . I never thought she'd choose *that* spot. It doesn't seem right to me for her to be giving birth on pictures of a bunch of naked women . . ."

"Don't worry. Mugs doesn't know the difference. She obviously feels safe in your room, right there under that table near your bed. She feels safe and she doesn't read . . ."

"Don't look at the pictures," he instructed me as we descended the stairs to his room.

"It's nothing I haven't seen before . . ."

"Mom!" Stephen drew away to reprimand me. "It's not the right thing for a mother to see."

For a quarter of our lives together we were lost to the other. Now an intimacy goes with us. Stephen sounds breathless when he calls my name and I answer in kind, as if the world retains something of the vastness across which we once saw the other disappearing.

When I wake at six each morning, there is often a note slipped under my door from Stephen. Sometimes the notes read: *Good morning, Mom. I hope you had a good night's sleep.*

Other times his notes request that I type the last half or proofread a paper he has written, due today, that he has left on my desk. In exchange for the favor he offers that he will walk the dogs this evening.

His notes alert me to observations he has made about the animals. *Dear Mom, I wanted you to know that Buster came down in the kitchen last night while you were asleep. He seemed twitchy so I gave him a Valium.* Or, *Dear Mom, Sybil came down into my room!* Or, *Sunny didn't come home last night...*

Once, when I was dating a man Stephen disliked, he left me a note that read, *Mother, to what chasm has your soul descended?*

Sometimes Stephen's notes go on for pages, his cramped, all-caps printing swimming before my eyes. He is worried about Trevor, or he and his girlfriend have had a fight. Or he's read or heard something he remembers in the night: *Mom, my teacher told me the greatest thing—if we seal all the windows in the house—really seal them up so no light gets through—we can actually turn the house into a camera. Isn't that the greatest?! Let's do it tomorrow...*

The morning of his eighteenth birthday his note reads, *Dear Mom, I know I won't be 18 until 3:07 P.M. (12:07 California time), but way to go, Mom! You had a handsome, brilliant, smart, stylish, amazingly exceptional baby boy!"*

Christmas night 1995. Clear. Very cold. We've driven
beyond the thin lights of Amherst into the country
where the stars have such presence they scare the atmosphere. I'm thinking of the ancients who divided
the night sky into the zodiac, like the twelve tribes of
Israel. It's as if the stories that overlay the stars, like Ja-
cob's curses and blessings of his sons, were attempts to
measure human terror against a vast and unpredictable
future.

The catalogue at the end of Genesis I once memorized
to win a prize at Sunday school comes back to me:

*Reuben, thou art my first born, my might, and the beginning
of my strength... Simeon and Levi are brethren: instruments
of cruelty are in their habitations... Dan shall be a serpent
by the way, an adder in the path, that biteth the horse's heels,
so that the rider shall fall backward...*

I've been waiting in the car for over an hour for Trevor, who has brought Christmas gifts to his mother, his younger sister and brothers. After walking him to the door and saying hello, I withdrew from the first reunion between Trev and his family. Trev touched my arm as I turned to go.

"Wait, please," he'd asked. "Don't leave."

"I'll be waiting in the car," I promised.

Keeping the engine running for the heat, flipping through radio stations, I listen here and there to carols, silly Christmas rock and roll, check my impatience with the idea that things must be going well, better than Trev expected.

Trevor's sadness and his silence have seemed to me nearly mythic at times. Never to learn a coherent narrative of his life before he came to live with us, I piece it together through the cold files of DYS, through witness and intuition, this combination of sources creating a tremendous need to try to protect him, act as his advocate and interpreter with the world, with school officials who have written him off, the probation officer who dispassionately checks off the date and enters another appointment, even the court-mandated therapist who comes to the house.

His approach is to try to be Trev's "pal," an affectation I could tell him will never work with this boy. Still, he persists, his "Hey, fellas" and his mixed metaphors and sports jargon booming throughout our rooms.

"The ball's in your court, man. Now it's up to you. You're a lucky fella, dude. Go for it. Whaddya say?"

Silence.

And yet more often now Trevor's beautiful deep baritone resonates as, alone in his room, he sings songs he has composed, his hands light on his drum. Other times Stephen creates back beats and mixes on his synthesizer over which Trevor freestyles.

Say that it's late. The backpacks full of schoolbooks sit unopened by the door. But I resist interrupting them, dragging them back to tasks and assignments that make them both feel like failures. Listening at the top of the basement stairs, I dwell in the heartbeat rhythms and the sweet sadness of the voice that gives them life.

Since Trev came to live with us I've thought about the New Testament parable of the Prodigal Son. I dig out my Bible to reread the story. But it's unsatisfying. In no way do I imagine that our house is like the house of the father. Nor is Trevor's fate like the Prodigal Son's. Trev's inheritance is one of longing. Can such an inheritance be squandered?

And where is the mother in the story? Doesn't she have a place in the house of God? How would her presence change things? Is she implicit in the psyche of the father who so generously calls his son home? When was she lost in the translation? I want to ask the translator. I want to touch the words in which she lived.

An old impertinence rises up in me, a frustration at text and culture. The scaffolds that surround the boys and me—the scaffolds of history, myth—show our fatherless household to be without a roof, or *built on sand.* The parable of the Prodigal Son erases the feminine without impunity. The mother in the story is at best assumed, insignificant to the outcome.

Or is God the father intended to be single? I am acquainted with a few single fathers in Amherst. With what
sympathy they are treated in the community. The assump-
tion inherent in such sympathy condemns the absent
mother as bad. How could she leave her husband and children? She is *unnatural.* Look at the hero the father. How
can the community help?

On the other hand the same community is wary of a
single-mothering household. Whether it be school officials, teachers, the march of probation officers, neighbors—each looks at our home and sees something missing.
I've heard it over and over from the factions who have entered our lives since Trevor moved in—that our household
lacks "structure, discipline."

"What Trevor needs," a neighbor once chastises
Stephen, "is strict monitoring, a rigorous schedule. Your
mother doesn't seem to understand this . . ."

What she means is that there is no father here, no man
to "complete" the picture. We are judged as not whole, as
wrong or crippled. All too often we are dealt with accord-
ingly—that is to say dismissed, unsavable for our lack,
doomed in our pursuits.

But where are the fathers? Not here on Christmas
night. Why aren't they here? They have new lives, new
wives, they have responsibilities. Believe them, they
would be here if they could. For this plea culture forgives
them. Soon, they say on the phone long distance. Say a
week this summer. Listen, they love their sons. Soon, they
promise.

I restart the engine and step on the gas to bring the
heat up. The lights of the apartment house in which

Trev's mother and siblings receive their gifts are cut almost brutally against the dark. What must Trev's mother be feeling tonight, her oldest son home for the first time in months? He wears his new Christmas jacket. And he has grown.

Maybe all I can offer Trevor is a few years off the streets and the distraction of a household he helped to create, a few years against eighteen, like the farm to which the Prodigal retreated during the famine and lived for a while until he *came to himself.*

Inside of Trevor's silence lives his right to privacy, his right to his own story if and when he sees fit to tell it. In the meantime I'll sit at the top of the basement steps and listen to his songs.

By now I've learned to read myself—woman and mother—relentlessly into the masculine, into the stories woven between the stars, or spun on earth: *And Zebulon shall dwell at the haven of the sea; and he shall be for an haven of ships...*

Only sometimes do I understand the crush of stories without us. Then we are light as a shadow, or radio static swarming the *Messiah*: . . . *unto us a son is given* . . .

But there are no fathers here.

Sybil / Photo by Stephen Digges

Nine A.M. of a weekday. Stephen is waiting his turn to
see the judge. As usual the Northampton courtroom is
crowded, the summoned and their parents, spouses, children, brothers and sisters standing, sitting. Every so often
a court official makes his way through the rows calling
out, "Any restraining orders! Restraining orders!" Some
women make their way toward the official and move out
the door.

The courtroom to which we've been assigned today is
less austere than others we've occupied. This one's a sort
of tired classroom with folding chairs skewed out of line.
We are knit close to our people, to family members,
lawyers.

There is little discussion between strangers, though at
the moment we have much in common. But the anatomy
of some personal crisis is soon to be made public, some
lightning-fast calamity of events that took place time and

distance from here, most likely in the dark; or events so plotted and executed they felt, however criminal—well, ordinary.

Now they are to be examined and dissected here in this unimpressive room under a fluorescence that drains color from faces and exaggerates every flaw. The air smells of coffee, anxious bodies, stale cigarette smoke clinging to hands, hair, coats, everyone drawn inward at the advent of exposure.

When we're mostly settled, a juvenile officer leads a line of boys, handcuffed and chained around their ankles, to the front pew. One of the boys scans the gallery for his mother, who sits next to us. Teary, she nods to him and shakes her head. I turn to her and catch her eyes.

"It'll be okay," I whisper. I have a sense that I'm invading her privacy, but I speak to her anyway. Likewise, Stephen engages her.

"Zeek's a friend of mine," he says. "He's a great kid."

As Stephen leans in front of me to quite directly comfort the woman, I can smell his cologne, his clean hair combed back neatly, his sweet breath. I'm not surprised by his spontaneous generosity, or his ease at breaking protocol. When he reaches for her hand, she responds.

"Thank you," she says. "You look real nice today," she adds, for the first time smiling a little.

"Not my usual." Stephen smiles back. He is wearing a suit and tie. He's removed his ear- and nose rings for the hearing—court appearance rituals of conduct he knows well.

The judge enters the courtroom; we rise, then resettle. The familiar anxiety that has ushered us to this moment now gives way to a resigned if not giddy anticipation of an ending. This is our fifth court appearance in two years, yes, *ours*. Against the conventional pop psychology that would suggest I *let Stephen deal with it alone ... let him experience the consequences of his actions without his mother holding his hand ... let him take his medicine ...*, I've escorted Stephen to each arraignment and hearing. I learned to hug him whether the ruling went for or against him, and to refrain from scolding.

I've learned that by keeping quiet, Stephen takes on his own remorse. In the absence of crowding him with advice and reprimands, he speculates on how to avoid such a situation again. *If you want to get to know someone,* say the Buddhists, *give him a big field to play in.*

Though to anyone else our presence here once again might appear just another dark chapter, it is actually a victory. Today's alleged offense involves a minor driving infraction complicated by the fact that Stephen seemed to have misplaced his driver's license.

In other words, there are no weapons involved, no one harmed, nothing missing, no property destroyed or defaced, no involvement of drugs or alcohol, no gang members waiting outside to grill Stephen regarding his possible implication of them, no resounding, lingering repercussions.

Just a simple, illegal left turn, a kid with a reputation and no driver's license on him, and a testy cop. We haven't engaged a lawyer. Stephen intends to speak for himself.

One by one, the cases are called. We know we might be here for hours. I've brought student essays to grade while we wait, Stephen his math homework. But by turns anxious, distracted, and bored, neither of us can concentrate.

We resort to our old ways, play many games of tic-tac-toe. Then we move on to a game Stephen invented a few court appearances back that involves finding—in one minute—as many words as possible in the other's name. When Stephen passes me his list with the word *boa* underlined next to a drawing of a woman with a snake around her neck, we almost lose our cool.

We are substantially into the inevitable Hangman—Stephen having stumped me regarding the category of rap group names, my little stick man now nearly complete with limbs, torso, head, though as yet no noose around the neck—when his case is called. It's close to eleven in the morning. Stephen practically leaps out of his seat and makes his way down to the bench where he stands before the judge, his head bowed, his hands folded in front of him.

"Mr. Digges," the judge begins after the charges are read.

"Yes, sir," Stephen answers.

"I've seen you here too many times."

"I know, sir. I'm sorry."

"I'm tired of seeing you here, Mr. Digges."

"Me, too, sir."

"You are speaking for yourself today?"

"I am."

"Very courageous. So tell me . . ."

Between them, Stephen and the judge review the violation. I strain to hear their discourse. Powerfully tempted to leave my seat and go to stand next to him, I check myself and observe my son for the first time alone before the judge as Stephen politely and thoroughly narrates.

I can't help thinking of the years that have brought us

here—hard years, surprising, devastating years, years during which we were torn and we tore raggedly, painfully from each other, our separation as physical, as passionate as our earliest connection as mother and son.

I smile at the irony as I imagine other parents feeling as I do at this moment, feeling pride as their son or daughter crosses the finish line to win the race, or kicks the ball hard to score the winning goal, or traverses the stage to receive some award, a moment in which they see their child as I see mine, separate and capable and worthy.

As for my Stephen, he seems to have been born for adversity, he who entered this world screaming, who loved to jump suddenly from a high stairs knowing someone would catch him, who'd run headlong at his mother just as later he would run headlong at the world, leaping on its back, wrestling it to the ground.

I suspect that were Stephen an animal, he'd be a blue jay, just as I've always thought that Charles and I would be sparrows.

So bandit-eyed, so undove like a bird . . . , Robert Francis writes in his poem "Blue Jay," a poem Stephen loved as a child. *Skulker and blusterer whose every arrival is a raid.*

In another life, Stephen might well have been one of those children who survived the war-torn ghettos by hiding out, scavenging, stockpiling food, growing strong in adversity, growing knowledgeable. Not so deep in Stephen's blood a wildness endures. *Good luck to the world*, I laugh to myself, *with Stephen in it.*

Now he is smiling as he makes his way back to me. "We can go," he whispers. "It's okay. Just a fine. I've brought my checkbook . . ."

We linger at the door as the boys on the front row are brought before the judge. Their legal counsel reviews the charges brought against them. Breaking and entering a private residence. Theft of guns and attempts to resell them. Assault with deadly weapons. Attempting to flee the scene of the crime in a stolen vehicle . . .

Zeek's mother makes her way to the bench to stand next to her son. She tries to remain composed. "Take him," she says when the judge allows her to speak. "Take him and take care of him or he'll be dead before his sixteenth birthday. I can't control him, Judge. I can't look after him . . ."

"Let's go." Stephen takes my arm. "Poor Zeek." He shakes his head. "He's gone. He's out of here . . ."

"Years, I'm afraid. What a shame."

"It was stupid what they did," Stephen says as we climb in the car. "They got caught up. Things lead to things. It's hard to stop it once it gets going. And it's *really* hard to pull out."

"I hear."

"I feel guilty, sort of."

"I can understand that."

"Zeek's just a kid."

"A lot younger than the others?"

"Ya. I've done some of the same things . . ."

"Hmm."

"He's just clueless."

"Well, maybe he's safer this way."

"Saf-er?"

"It's a hard call, isn't it?"

"I guess," he says, the flash of anger subsiding. "Look,

Mom." Stephen stops my hand as I begin to turn the key in the ignition. "Let's make a deal. Let's say we try never to come back here."

"Sounds good . . ."

"Well, not try . . . *there is no try*."

"Good old Yoda."

"How many years was I Yoda for Halloween?"

"Three?"

"So let's just say we *won't ever* come back here."

"Okay."

"We should shake on it."

"Okay, let's shake."

"Deal?"

"Deal."

* * *

PERSONAL STATEMENT / STEPHEN DIGGES

Throughout my high school career, much of my extracur-
ricular experience in the arts and the social sciences has
been of my own invention. This is because my interests in
music, photography, poetry, and psychology have tended to
be nontraditional. While my school has offered me opportu-
nities in talent shows, the darkroom, and the classroom (I
made the honor roll this year), I have independently set up
my own means of practicing my art by creating my own
music studio and darkroom.

I have also contracted, this year, to complete an internship
with Amherst psychologist Eduardo Bustamante, whose work
focuses on spirited children who cannot learn in traditional
settings. Under Dr. Bustamante's guidance I have worked
with and helped to counsel ADD and ADHD children. Using
Dr. Bustamante's Play and Pride approach, I am completing

From *The Broken Composition* / Photos by Stephen Digges

my own studies on my observations of new ways for children with frontal-lobe deficiencies to be challenged and successful. Not only have I been proud to assist Dr. Bustamante, but this project has been extremely helpful to me as a person with ADD. I, too, have had trouble learning in the highly traditional setting of public school. Working and reading and writing on the subject have given me confidence in my own nontraditional ways of learning. I believe that I have also given confidence and insight to those who are struggling with some of the same problems I have faced at school.

My family and I have also traveled extensively, so once again, my "classroom" has been the world. My family and I lived in London for two years prior to my attending Amherst Regional High School. Attending the American School in London, I interacted with classmates from all over the world. I have also traveled to Italy and Holland. My visit to Amsterdam I planned myself; this December, for the first time, I set out without parents to explore the Netherlands.

Last summer I traveled to New York to be a student at Parsons School of Design Summer Intensive Program in Photography. This experience above all others has led me to know that what I want to do with my life is to be a photojournalist, be out in the world with my camera. The Parsons project I invented for myself was to interview individuals who are homeless and to ask their permission to be photographed. I completed a photographic essay on these individuals in a book of my own creation entitled The Broken Composition. It is my ambition to expand this project and, along with my photographs, carefully and articulately narrate the stories of those who so willingly shared with me their experiences.

Stephen P. Digges

DEBORAH DIGGES

To: Amherst Building Inspector

Description of work done on conversion of two-car garage (length) into study (back) and summer porch/room (front) at 101 Blue Hills Road:

Back of garage was made into a study in 1992 by my former husband, Stanley Plumly, who took ownership of the house at that time.

He did much of the work himself and, from what I understand, did not know that he must have a permit to fix up the back portion of the garage. Over the course of several years, he insulated the room himself and hired someone to wire the room as well as install a wall heater.

E. T., a builder, helped with Sheetrocking the ceilings. Stanley Plumly also had indoor/outdoor carpeting put in.

I talked to him recently on the phone about it and he estimated that all the materials he bought or had in his possession cost around three thousand dollars. At the time of the back room's completion, the front of the garage remained unfinished.

Stanley Plumly has not resided at the above address since 1993. At our divorce, I was given the house.

I have not refinanced, because I would have had to do so at a much higher interest rate. I am forwarding to the Town of Amherst a copy of our divorce decree so that it can be shown that the house is legally mine.

*Front of garage was converted in 1995. My own son and my
foster son painted the walls and ceilings and I installed a ceiling fan. E. T. helped us with four skylights and put a wall with
door and window up where we had taken out the garage door.*

*We also set up an old woodstove I had bought at a garage
sale which now is used as a planter. E. T. put in the chimney
but advised us not to use the stove since it would need a fire-
wall behind it. Stove has plants on and around it.*

*In the spring of 1996 I had indoor/outdoor carpeting put in
and tile installed under the stove that matched tile in the en-
tryway. The cost of putting up the wall where the garage
door had been, plus the cost of the skylights, carpeting, tile,
etc., came to about three thousand dollars.*

*Thus, I am including eighty-five dollars to be sure to cover
everything. If there are any additional adjustments, please
contact me since I am willing to do whatever is necessary
for this work to be sanctioned and permissible to the Amherst Building Inspector.*

Sincerely...

**LETTER OF RECOMMENDATION FOR STEPHEN P. DIGGES
10 JAN. 1996**

*I have known Stephen for the past four years, first through
his interest in—and affection for—animals, and then more
generally I came to know him and his family (his mother is*

a professor at Tufts University, where I was dean of veterinary medicine for nearly fourteen years before moving to Cornell last fall).

Steve is one of the most interesting and creative youngsters I have come to know. He is particularly interested in the cultural and emotional dimensions of factual material. Animals interested him initially because of their ability, in his eyes, to express "feelings" in particular situations. Later he came to become interested in their behavior and when his talent for photography emerged, he applied this to animals and other parts of the natural world.

He is what I would describe as a "non-linear" learner; he makes observations anecdotally, then merges them over time into a coherence that makes order out of the whole. Thus, he is a talented maker of music using synthesizers, photographs using multiple images (often superimposed), and unusual vocabulary words.

Clearly I am not a professional in the area of the arts, but Stephen is a very special person, and I have dealt with people his age for over thirty years. I believe him to have a special dedication to and talent for the creative arts in a way I've not previously encountered. And he is extremely caring in his dealings with other people and, of course, with animals.

Franklin M. Loew
Dean
Cornell Veterinary College

Corrections and changes for Rough Music.

1. See acknowledgments page: Note that the poem initially titled "The Afterlife" has been changed to "Chekhov's Darling." The acknowledgment Ploughshares *should read "Chekhov's Darling" under the title "The Afterlife."*

2. See dedication page: Note that the name Frank has been added to the dedication. Thus, the dedication should read: "For Stephen and Charles, for Trevor, and Susan, and Gerry, and Max, and for Frank."

3. See table of contents page: The title of "The Afterlife" has been changed to "Chekhov's Darling" (17th poem).

4. See "Late Summer," page 6. Note correction in line 23. "Theresa" has been corrected to "Therese."

5. See page 12, second page of "Rune for the Parable of Despair." In line 6 of the second page, note that the word "blessed" has been put in quotation marks.

6. See page 15, line 17 of "Rough Music." There should be a hyphen between "breaking" and "glass." It should read "breaking-glass."

7. See page 32, "Morning After a Blizzard." Drop the "And" that begins the poem. It should read, "What could they possibly need to bury in heaven?"

8. See page 36, "Five Smooth Stones." The first letter of line 12 should be capitalized since it is the beginning of a new

DEBORAH DIGGES

sentence. It should read, "He walks the streets opening gates
for the yard dogs ..."

9. See page 38. Change title of poem from "The Afterlife"
to "Chekhov's Darling."

At line five break line at the word "raised."
Add a dash after the word "pain."
Omit the lines, "like Chekhov's and it was clear to them the
end was still far off ..."

Chekhov's Darling

Then came the day even the water glass felt heavy
and I knew, as I'd suspected, I grew lighter.
I grew lighter, yes.
Say, have you ever fainted?
Such a distinct horizon as you are raised above your pain:
And after forty years they entered Canaan ...
Don't tell me about turning from what might change you,
taking the second, not the first compartment
in the revolving door,
tossing the note in the bottle back into the channel.
No, the afternoon was not a practice for another.
The birds, they flew.
The virus spread throughout the city.
It was a real day and I grew lighter.
And I asked my friend if I could hold his arm
to keep myself from rising.
I picked up the rare city stones and put them in my pocket
while the buildings dreamed themselves
backwards to rubble, and the sun-smashed

windows, the mortar back to sand,
and Orpheus in the flesh set broken china
into the fissures of the sidewalk after he'd poured the grout
and smoothed it with his trowel.
Then blue shard by blue shard he made a sky of the abysmal
sepulchers across which the homeless
floated, much as I, where
the trains passed, and the ground shook.
It was like standing inside singing, knowing something of its
need.
It was the troubled child grown old, happy, the lost in sight
of home, and born for this.
There is a sadness older than its texts
that will outlive the language,
like the lover who takes you by the roots of your hair.
In this way I was awake, I was light,
I grew lighter,
though I had not yet been lifted.

* * *

If you had to describe *house* to an alien, you might begin
with ours. It would be a simple lesson drawn in the dirt
with a stick: a rectangle with smaller ones inside, front
entrance, dining room to the left, living room to the right,
kitchen along the back. Upstairs is as simple: two bedrooms separated by a bathroom off the landing.

Behind the house the woods bear in, shrinking the yard
a little more this year, ferns and saplings sprouting from
the leaf piles dumped over the fence, fallen tree branches
from an ice storm dragged back and heaved over, weeds,
dead bushes pulled out of the ground, bulbs that rotted in
the window boxes, dead tomato plants, vase after vase of
wild flowers thrown out, Christmas trees dumped, debris
piling up, seeded and seeding, spilling over.

It's a house easily lost in green or memory. Such is
its effaced dignity, a postwar modesty tinged with shame
regarding exposed cinderblock foundations, aluminum

siding, low ceilings, unadorned windows, door frames, staircase, fireplace. Were it to disappear, fall in or sail off one night, neighbors walking their dogs might say, "Wasn't there a house there among the trees? Maybe. Or maybe we were mistaken."

It's a house aware of New England's weathers, the changing light altering the interiors as if it wanted to be a different house each season. By summer it stars the upper rooms among treetops. The boys climb out the windows to sit on the roof overlooking the woods where they sun themselves, drink iced coffee.

Winters we live downstairs in front of the fire. Then with the spring thaw the basement floods, soaking this or that box of books and photos we carry up the bulkhead and mete out, pinning pictures to the clothesline, saving as many as we can, throwing the rest away, not without relief.

Our animals bring in the weathers. By now we have nine cats and three dogs who smell of the grass, the autumn leaves, smell of rain, dust, pinesap. Spring, summer, and fall the cats bring their kills into the house—mice, voles, birds. This morning I woke to find a sleek star-nosed mole on my pillow.

Stephen has rescued a kangaroo mouse from Vasco, by far the most gifted hunter. Stephen resuscitated the mouse by rubbing its throat and belly, and kept the mouse as a pet in his old hamster cage. He named him Frederick, who seemed happy to be protected through the winter. By spring he escaped his cage, though we see him now and then around the house, nearly sauntering toward the kitchen.

The cat we call Mr. T. once caught a wood thrush and carried it up to Trevor's room. We discovered Mr. T. and her bird apparently resting together, the bird alert, quiet in its wisdom, Mr. T. lounging next to it. Trevor carefully, stealthily lifted the bird from between Mr. T.'s paws and delivered it outside. It sat on Trevor's finger a few moments, then flew up into the mountain ash where it chirped and crabbed, furious for the near-fatal adventure.

The wide backyard slopes toward the woods, the hillside covered with pine needles on which G.Q. likes to slide on his back. He slides under the huge white pine, the hammock strung between trees, slides toward what will be his own burial ground when, later this year, he'll suddenly have a stroke, his epitaph to read *Earth, receive an honored guest...*

But from this April window today I can still watch him, Rufus, Buster, and some of the cats as they lounge in the new grass near the woods. Stephen and Trevor have dragged lawn chairs down there and they sun themselves among their brood.

I love those animals who lie so peacefully around my boys. I'm grateful for the many times they have drawn the boys away from anger, sadness. They've taught us in ways only animals can; their muteness insists that we listen with eyes and hearts. We lived blessed in our speculations.

The animals offer us a subject besides ourselves, besides the frustration of human interaction, work, scheduling, bad tempers, fatigue. They become our higher concern, need care and attendance in spite of run-ins with

the law, missed classes, failing grades, flat tires, snow-
storms, the furnace on the blink, the refrigerator empty.
Care of the animals, above all, is what we come to value
in one another. To defer to and care properly for them in
the midst of crisis is to be a success, to be praised and
cherished.

We mirror our animals and they us. Buster mirrors us
in his sudden shifts to seizing. We must stop what we are
doing and come to his aid. Stripping off the urine-soaked
sheets, our T-shirts smeared with feces, we make peace
with our own helplessness as we practice a tolerance of
a kind we hadn't believed ourselves capable.

As for G.Q., we now know he can't help his aggression
that looks to all the world like meanness. Having forgiven
him, we must still be consistent in our work with him and
make sure he gets his medicine as we learn how difficult
it is for all of us in this house to practice restraint.

And Rufus? Who could have imagined that the leveret-
killing Rufus would so passionately nurture our orphaned
kittens? Who could have predicted that he was just the
dog for the job? What quality in him was stirred, not only
to lick down the kittens, but to climb into the drawer after each feeding and settle among them, providing them
with his closeness, warmth?

A new cat has found us. Maybe from the woods she saw
our light, or followed the others to see where they retreated each night. For weeks last winter we set food on
the sill and kept the kitchen window open, though it was
below freezing outside, our fifty-year-old furnace pump-
ing up heat day and night in deference to her, the second
floor a balmy eighty degrees.

After a while she came halfway in the window. By moving her food to the counters we got her to come inside. Soon she took up residence behind the couch. She grew fat and healthy, fighting with the other cats if they approached her, hissing and striking out if the dogs dared to pass too close.

The boys named her Sybil because one moment she craved affection and in the next batted them away with open claws. Trevor worked hardest at taming her. He'd lie on the floor by the couch, cooing, coaxing her. Opening cans of tuna, he'd mete out treats for her, at the same time tossing chunks to the dogs to keep them at bay.

One day Stephen discovered Sybil preening herself in the loft of our newly converted garage. He called Trevor, Charles, and me to the threshold to see. Stephen took Sybil's picture and developed it. Now it's mounted on our fridge, a trophy for Trevor in honor of what he's made possible.

May, 1996
Stephen Digges
Expository Writing
Prose poem narrative

Body Music

Clouds muted the light that day. Shadows drifted away from their human mirrors, parting companions. Dulled. March rain touched the children's faces in schoolyards. I watched them in passing. The moisture clung to everyone's skin. Wind chimes sounded, like too many navigations into the wet morning air. I walked listening.

My destination was unknown, but it was a path of meander intricately spinning itself while I walked, a giant loom unraveling at my feet. Missouri. In the thawing ponds and lakes carp fed on neurolichen. I felt twisted, ashamed of my existence.

An old man sat in a chair on a white porch in front of his time-dusted, one-story house. He watched me through his "wisdom": I met his eyes below the brim of his brown mesh baseball cap that read "Smith & Wesson."

Now beyond his vision, I still felt his eyes judging me. The day was repeating itself.

Missouri had trapped me inside it, trapped me inside my father's home. It was as if I had tripped, my step thrown off, and now I was destined to walk in circles for what felt like the eternity of my thirteenth year.

The past was useless rhetoric. My life in the city had become irrelevant, though like the end of a song sequence, the memory directed my every stride—. My body still moved with it, that period of my life in which I had lived as a dreamer on Boston's streets.

In comparison Columbia, Missouri, was the stopped time of neon malls, golf courses, duplexes, trailer parks, and cow pastures. This was my new residence.

The short time I had already spent in Missouri was miserable. Only two weeks at my new school, West Junior High, had passed before the principal called me into her office. Her voice twanged with a deep southern accent. She spoke sternly through tight lips.

"I know why you're here, Stephen. Your father and I had a long chat about it before I let you into this school..."

My ears would not listen anymore and my eyes became blank windows watching her, while my mind took me to other places, my real home, my mother, and the scent of spray paint freshly drying on the outdoor walls of Boston.

"Are you even listening to me, Stephen?" she interrupted my reverie.

"Yeah, yeah, I am," I responded softly, gazing now on the floor.

"Have we reached an understanding then?" she inquired.

"*Most likely,*" *I retorted. She didn't take my answer well. She began dissecting my appearance.*

"*And if you think you can go around this school with pants hangin' half off your ass, an' a bad attitude, you're wrong, Mr. Digges. An' next time I see you wearin' your pants like that I am gonna wrap a rope around your waist, and make you wear it all day. This school has a dress code an'...*" *Droplets of spit flew from her lips as she pronounced her s's.*

Tears began to blur my vision, rounding the world into one narrow tunnel. I wasn't quite sure why, but I felt like a silhouette, half human, all details fading. My life had become so foreign, an interrupted, irregular maze that bore sharp edges, the shapes becoming more and more abstract with each tick of the seconds inside of Central Standard Time.

After that exchange with the principal, I had set out on my wandering at ten-thirty in the morning. I had left silently, hiding my emotions so that the principal wouldn't detect how powerfully she had got to me.

The path found itself and I followed it. Ten miles from my father's house I stepped left after right, in a silent fury. The white, one-story houses all looked the same, distinguished by junked cars that littered the lawn, a brown sofa leaking tan innards at the arm rests, on the cushions, bed mattresses stained with rust from the springs that coiled toward the sky like useless promises.

And it was on this street that the old man in his rifle cap had scrutinized and judged me. "Someday he'll choke," I thought, "on this Missouri air."

As for the boy the old man shook his head at, now I

recall him for you, recall the boy to let him go, and
wish the past well, five years later. If I were to have met
him/myself on that day of wandering, I would tell
him to be patient, to love his individuality, to listen to
the answers that lie within, that come in the tempos
and waves of the heartbeat. Just listen and wait. Body
music.

Grade: B+

Hadwen Park. I'm walking the dogs through a woods
south of Worcester. It's late October, warm enough I
hardly need a jacket. Most of the leaves are down, the
paths along the steep hillsides lost under the eddying
leaves, pine needles.

The dogs run out ahead, debris parting in their wake,
and as I walk I kick aside the leaves to read the graffiti
strewn across the asphalt. Names, insults, professions of
love, and the names of rock and rap bands, Nirvana, The
Dead, framed by marijuana leaves.

As I head down the hill I cross the blue-black outline
of a huge penis and testicles, more names, apparently
of a more recent era for the names of the bands, the
pitched tenor of the profanities, as if the older graffiti
had somehow been a draft for this great black smear like
a cloud or a thought, across which is written, in white,
school sucks.

"School sucks," I say as I align myself in the old exercise of joining, which Eduardo once taught me so well. School sucks, and all its horrors of restriction. And its teachers suck, who are surely aliens sent to torture their students with rules, deadlines, information that the kids believe has so little to do with their lives.

Kids' lives are on fire, and Mr. So-and-so says they have to do math. Their lives are burning and Ms. ———— says that paper is due tomorrow, no hats in the house, no smoking, four minutes between classes.

School sucks that houses their days, children in the throes of adolescence that does violence to the body and soul, that is the world changing while they are not, or vice versa, the world in wrong alignment. How to navigate the chasm?

Both Trevor and Stephen made it through, each in his way. After our battling the administration as we futilely tried to see to his advancement, Trevor made the decision to drop out of high school. He successfully took his GEDs in the fall of his sixteenth year and began junior college. Taking a job at a Caribbean restaurant in Amherst, he moved out of our house to share an apartment with friends in June of 1996, the spring of Stephen's graduation. The following fall, Stephen began a B.F.A. in photography in New York City.

We celebrated Stephen's graduation. His father and grandparents flew in from Missouri, and Stanley came up from Maryland. Charles, who had moved back to Russia in January of 1996 to work as a journalist, returned to see his brother graduate. Charles brought with him many friends who had known Stephen in Brookline, and who, over the years, came to understand the portent of the event.

Trevor returned for the celebration, bringing with him jerk chicken and beans for the party we threw the next day. My sister Eve drove up from Connecticut to help prepare for the all-day event we planned for Stephen, his guests, and his friends.

A subtext of possibilities went unspoken. But the alternative story with its different trajectory ghosted, even intensified our celebration. It offered that Stephen's graduation from high school was not *the* moment that he and we who loved him had been waiting for.

Rather, it was *a* moment, like so many others, which made one kind of future more immediately accessible than another. We were not unaware of the other grueling, even tragic alternative. Inside that alternative we glimpsed ourselves as flat, dismissible characters—the helpless single mother and the rebellious teen—roles reinforced by a culture pointing fingers at us, roles that separated a son from his mother and isolated us in our confusion.

That culture judged me harshly while it allowed my young son, lost in adolescent grief, easy access to guns. Stephen's graduation from high school exemplified our tenuous connection to a system that insisted on itself as the only way, though we knew it was not the only way at all. Trevor had taught us that, and Eduardo, and our animals.

Under the circumstances, Zeek's mother's pleas in District Court that day, pleas for the judge to take him— yes—put him in jail *or he'll be dead before his sixteenth*

birthday . . . , might be a way, too, to see a child safely
through the dark regions of adolescence.

I follow the dogs into the woods toward the river,
meeting as we go other dogs and their people, meeting
kids, who in spite of the warmth, wear ball caps and huge
jackets over their baggy jeans. It's midday, a weekday.
They've probably skipped school. The boys stop to watch
my dogs dive into the river to retrieve the sticks I throw.
They hold cigarettes down close to their sides, wary that
I might be someone they know, or someone who knows
them.

"Want to throw one?" I offer.

"Na-a," one answers, taking a nervous drag from his
smoke. But they linger awhile watching the dogs run
headlong into the water to leap and swim, then charge up
the hill to drop the sticks at my feet, eager, shaking water
everywhere as they insist on another plunge.

Where have the kids to go, anyway? The day is huge,
full of distance and light, all the leaves down, and time
seems odd inside such brilliance, something at its periph-
eries insisting, parents, teachers, cops at the edge of the
light, but just now at the edge merely. Such light burns
out memory, burns out the autumns of their childhoods,
what that felt like. And what now feels like they scrawl
across the asphalt.

What now will feel like later is as hard to say.

And as for how later will look back at now—who
knows? The jury, as my sister and I used to say to each
other, is still out. Indeed it is out—the jury is having dinner in a restaurant, then going to the opera, or it has
boarded a plane, or it loads its trunks onto a ship, drags

great "Bon Voyage" wreaths up the gangplank, then appears at the rail to wave back at us as the ship backs out of the harbor.

The jury is blessedly out on all of us, and if and when it comes in with its verdict, let's hope that we've grown up, that we've escaped, somehow, that we've beat it into years in which life appears to make sense, years in which we finally, for the first time, catch up to ourselves, and that the charges brought against us long ago, in that other life—that other strange life in which we were a blur to ourselves and to the ones who loved us—are forgivable.

The dogs run off into the wide lap of the hillside, chase squirrels up trees then dash into underbrush. Now Rufus is the oldest among the three, fit and healthy at eight years old. Buster died a few years ago, and G.Q. They lie buried in our yard in Amherst.

Last summer Charles gave me my shepherd-husky mix, a stray female I named Annie. And Max the dalmatian was Stephen's gift to me just after Buster died. Max had belonged to the super of Stephen's apartment building in New York. After Stephen's first year in school he moved out of the dorms and into Alphabet City. His super bought the dalmatian as a puppy for his daughter, but the dog grew up, as dalmatians tend to do, big and unruly and loud. His barking and whining from the basement troubled Stephen. He convinced the super to let him take Max home to Amherst.

As for our cats, Frank and I have Einstein and Vasco with us in Worcester, the other four living in Amherst. Those four were born in the house and grew up hunting

the woods behind. Sybil is among them. Frank and I
drive out from Worcester several times a week. We
are together now. Often the cats come in through the
kitchen window to greet us and to partake in our re-
filling of their huge vats of cat food. Sometimes we
find mice, voles, bits of wing on the kitchen floor.

I say good-bye to the kids who still stand, awkward,
smoking, shifting their weight from one foot to the
other.

"Nice dogs," one of them says to me.

"Thanks," I answer. "You guys be good."

They shrug as they head up the steep path toward the
street, then down the wide drive, perhaps over their own
handiwork. They wear that slump-shouldered luckless
look I recognize, but when Max dashes back to circle and
sniff them, their faces wake to a boyishness and one of
them turns to wave to me.

In that gesture I see him so completely that I
glimpse my Stephen. The day I took him to college we
waited in lines, dragged his trunk up to his dorm room,
made up his bed. And then he was ready for me to go.
He walked me down to the car, double-parked on a busy
street.

"Now don't forget to take your vitamins," I'd said.

"Don't worry, Mom . . ."

"And you know, take it easy, take it slow . . ."

"I'll be fine . . ."

"This is New York," I'd warned.

"I know!" He'd grinned.

Stephen opened the car door for me. We hugged one
more time and then he dashed back across the street.

"Be careful on the way home!" he called above the traffic as he turned to wave to me.

"And Mom!" he shouted, breaking into a wide grin, shaking his head at my tears. "You'll be okay, Mom!" he called. "Take good care of the animals! And Mom, listen! Thanks for a wonderful childhood!"